THE

ILLUSTRATED HISTORY OF WEAPONS

KNIVES
DAGGERS
& HAND-COMBAT TOOLS

KINGSFORDEDITIONS

Distributed by Kingsford Editions
45–55 Fairchild Street
Heatherton Victoria 3202 Australia
www.hinkler.com.au

Copyright © Hinkler Books Pty Ltd 2014

Created by Moseley Road Inc.
President: Sean Moore
Project art and editorial director: Tina Vaughan and Damien Moore
Cover design: Hinkler Design Studio
Internal design: Andy Crisp, Lisa Purcell,
Philippa Baile and Mark Johnson-Davies
Photographer: Jonathan Conklin Photography, Inc.
f-stop fitzgerald
Author: David Soud
Prepress: Graphic Print Group

ISBN: 978 1 7436 3059 4

Printed and bound in China

THE
ILLUSTRATED HISTORY OF WEAPONS
KNIVES DAGGERS
& HAND-COMBAT TOOLS

David Soud

KINGSFORD EDITIONS

Contents

Introduction:
The Way of the Knife

The dagger is the most intimate of weapons. It is worn close to the body, often concealed. Its use requires its wielder to be within an arm's length of his adversary at most, and often much closer. And it is powerfully ambiguous as a symbol, at once bespeaking the courage of close combat, the heightened atmosphere of ritual sacrifice, and the treachery of murder and assassination. Shakespeare's Macbeth is a heroic soldier when he cleaves enemies in two with his sword; when he first envisions and then takes up a dagger, he becomes a murderer. Hamlet contemplates suicide with a dagger in hand, but accomplishes his revenge mission with a sword. Countless assassinations have been effected with pugios, stilettos, rondels, baselards, ballock knives, combat knives, and other iterations of the basic dagger form: a short, acute blade, usually double-edged, attached to a handle.

The earliest daggers were, of course, made of stone or bone. They were the closest a human being could get to the sharp claw of a born predator, but they doubtless found immediate use in self-defense, treachery, or open combat with other human beings. Already in the Stone Age, tremendous care and the most advanced available technologies went into the crafting of blades; as far back as 70,000 BCE, the earliest smiths were heat-treating selected stones to make them flake under precisely applied pressure into sharper, more attractive edges. The subsequent technologies of copper, bronze, iron, and steel all had a great deal to do with the need for keener, stronger, more resilient blades.

In an age where warfare has become, for the most part, impersonal and abstract, the dagger and fighting knife have taken on a halo of nostalgia. To confront an

GREENSTONE CELT

This celt, from North America, is made from greenstone. A very hard rock found in riverbeds, greenstone is hard to work, but its durability is similar to that of iron. While this celt was used as a woodworking tool, it and similar blades are the early ancestors of weapons like the battle-axe.

ROMAN DAGGER

A Roman military dagger, or pugio, dating from the Imperial period and unearthed at Oberstimm in Germany. This impressive weapon is a smaller version of a gladius, or Roman short sword. The blade is most suitable for stabbing, but can also be used for slashing. The cruciform guard and balanced pommel set the pattern for the arming swords of Medieval Europe.

enemy with a knife forces some acknowledgement of his humanity even in the effort to disable or kill him; he is no longer an idea, a distant target, or a blip on a radar screen. It is true that for most of the history of warfare, the dagger has been the weapon of last resort. In the ancient world, especially in Central Asia, fighting distances were measured at most in the length of an arrow's flight. For the soldiers of Greece and Rome, the spear was the primary weapon, and the sort of melee in which one would draw a short sword or dagger signified a breakdown in a military formation, or the closing stages of a battle. But this very intimacy has also made the dagger a badge of courage and honor. A Sioux warrior could only "count coup" by engaging an enemy closely enough to reach out and touch him. To have fought with a knife is to have fought in the most primordial sense.

FLINT DAGGER, GERMANY

A well-preserved flint knife dating to 2900 BCE, found near Allensberg, Germany, where a Neolithic settlement was excavated by Lake Constance. The blade is, like all knapped stone blades, serrated, and the blade profile is suited to piercing as well as slicing. Note how the wooden handle has been preserved, revealing the practical mountings of such sharp stone blades.

SHANG DYNASTY BRONZE KNIFE

Shang Dynasty knife, broad blade and substantial hilt, which might also have been mounted as a dagger-axe, has a single-edged blade with substantial heel and bolster, and a pistol-shaped hilt carved with geometric designs that may have been inlaid with turquoise.

Technology Meets Design

Although all knives are potentially deadly weapons, some are clearly designed specifically for violence, while others are constructed as tools or have a more symbolic function. Certain European stilettos, for example, seem made solely for the purpose of murder; centuries of history, art, and literature have endowed such weapons with dark associations. At the same time, many Mughal daggers are magnificent works of art, and seem fashioned to elicit admiration rather than be put to any practical purpose. The Indonesian *kriss* is often a fearsome-looking weapon, but it lacks that hint of explosive violence that can seem to inhabit some Bowie knives, or the occult strangeness that surrounds an Aztec sacrificial blade.

In the Bronze Age, the dagger took on many variations of its archetypal theme. Bronze may not hold an edge or sustain stress as well as iron or steel, but it is much more easily worked, and the Bronze Age smiths of Luristan, in what is now northern Iran, conjured a variety of blades and fitted them with often intricately cast mountings. Some of those weapons suggest cultural interchange with early China, where inlays of precious stones often adorned bronze blades. The Dong Son and other cultures of Southeast Asia became expert in bronze metalworking as well. In Egypt, where iron ore was scarce, bronze daggers remained the norm into the Iron Age. Bronze blades unearthed in Greece, especially those of Mycenae, have remarkably expert and vivid decorative inlays of gold and other materials.

When iron-smelting technology came to the fore, those cultures that had access to the best-quality ore

BOWIE STYLE KNIFE

A 20th-century European knife fashioned in the style of the classic American Bowie knife, with an acute clip-point blade. The pistol-shaped grip is an interesting twist on a classic design, and the brass-trimmed hardwood sheath is exceptionally fine.

DONG SON DAGGER

5th-century BCE dagger of the Dong Son culture, which flourished in what is now northern Vietnam in the last millennium BCE. The Dong Son people were expert bronze casters—their bronze drums were traded throughout East and Southeast Asia—and that expertise is evident in this fine weapon, which has a distinctive hilt design and blade profile.

IBERIAN DAGGER

An iron dagger from Iberia, c. 450–200 BCE, unearthed in what is now Andalusia, in southern Spain. In form, the blade follows classic Roman design, with a broad base that tapers to an acute tip. The hilt includes a sturdy bolster and a winged pommel suggestive of the antenna swords and knives of some Celtic cultures.

tended to produce the finest blades. In Europe, this was especially true of Iberia. The Iron Age blades produced in what is now Spain were much sought after before and during the Roman era; in fact, their superior blades were key to the long-successful resistance by some Iberian tribes to Roman expansion in the region. The classic Iberian dagger, with a triangular blade, became an iconic weapon during the last few centuries BCE. The Iberian tradition of fine blades would continue well into the modern era, with Toledo in particular being one of the great knife-making centers of Europe, rivaled only by Solingen in Germany and Sheffield in England.

But the knife blade found its ideal materials in India and Japan. India was the origin of wootz steel, an alloy used for the production of the legendary "watered steel" or Damascus blades that have become some of the most sought-after in history. For centuries, the finest blades of India, Persia, and the great Islamic empires were crafted of this steel, which contained a distinctive array of impurities and was forged into blades through a process that left unmistakable organic patterns on the finished blade surface. Unfortunately, knowledge of that process was lost by the end of the 18th century. To this day, Damascus steel remains the Holy Grail of blade-making. Researchers try and fail to recreate it. Contemporary knifemakers use the word "Damascus" to describe conventionally pattern-welded blades, which do not even approach the extraordinary combination of strength, resilience, and edge-holding power of true Damascus.

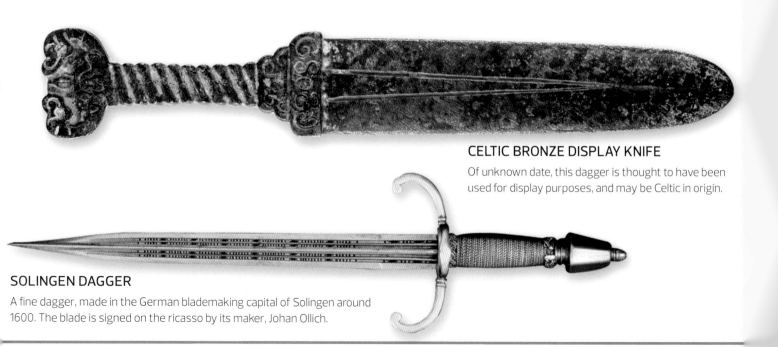

CELTIC BRONZE DISPLAY KNIFE

Of unknown date, this dagger is thought to have been used for display purposes, and may be Celtic in origin.

SOLINGEN DAGGER

A fine dagger, made in the German blademaking capital of Solingen around 1600. The blade is signed on the ricasso by its maker, Johan Ollich.

The Dagger as Art Object

In Japan, as in some other cultures, traditional blades are regarded as infused with spirit, and they are forged in a highly ritualized way. Toward the end of the 1st millennium CE, the Japanese perfected the process of layering and differentially hardening steel, investing that process with the highly aesthetic sensibility that has always characterized Japanese culture. The resulting blades have a streamlined, beautifully formed elegance, and connoisseurs appreciate even the smallest details of their form and composition.

This aestheticization of the dagger blade has, in every knife-making tradition, extended to its mountings. The sheaths and handles of Japanese daggers are themselves often exquisite works of art, rendered in such materials as gilt copper, silver, ivory, and especially the natural lacquer known as urushi, which polishes to a vibrant and durable finish while creating endless decorative possibilities, especially when combined with gold inlay or brushwork in what is called maki-e. The daggers of the Mughal Empire offer a different but equally refined aesthetic, their handles in particular often expertly carved and polished from jade, agate, or other precious materials, and tastefully inlaid with precious metals and stones. Such radiant hilts were often fitted with Damascus blades, beautifully inlaid with ornamental patterns. Inlay also figures widely in the knives of the various Islamic cultures, many of which overlap with much older traditions of the dagger. Islamic blades often feature exquisite damascening, typically in arabesque patterns and Arabic calligraphy.

The Western aestheticization of the dagger involved some of the same techniques, combined with native traditions. After the early Medieval period, when the dagger seemed to have fallen out of wide use, it returned to favor around the 12th century and became an art object as well as a weapon. Though form usually followed function—the sword-hilt dagger, rondel, baselard, and ballock knife all had practical elements—ornament became increasingly important.

SWISS DAGGER WITH EXQUISITE SCABBARD

An early 16th-century Swiss dagger with a magnificent sheath. The sheath reveals how a Renaissance dagger could be used as a statement of status and taste. Because the dagger would be worn horizontally in its owner's belt, the intricate gold-plated openwork on the sheath "reads" along the axis of the blade.

During the Renaissance, when swords became more problematic for civilian use—sumptuary laws often barred most classes from wearing them—dress daggers were adopted as means of both self-defense and self-display. The dagger was a fashion accessory, and famed sculptors and artists were commissioned to design their mountings. By the middle to late 19th century, when Romanticism invoked nostalgic and stylized visions of the Middle Ages and early Renaissance, the dagger had taken two distinct forms: the Romantic art object and the fighting knife. Only the officer's daggers of the European militaries bridged that divide.

The 20th- and 21st-century dagger has continued to follow that dual path. There is a vast market in expensive collector's knives made of exotic hardwoods and precious metals, often with pattern-welded blades. Combat daggers, sometimes highly traditional but more often of high-tech materials in lightweight designs, have grown ever more popular.

But the fundamental mystique of the dagger remains. It is the original bladed weapon, with tens of thousands of years of history behind it. And it remains both a practical implement and a potent symbol.

CLOISONNÉ DAGGER AND SHEATH

An example of a highly decorated knife and sheath dating from the 19th century. Cloisonné enamel has been used on both the hilt and sheath.

CHINESE DAGGER

A 19th-century Chinese dagger, with a typically curved blade and a beautifully carved bone sheath.

Before Metal Blades

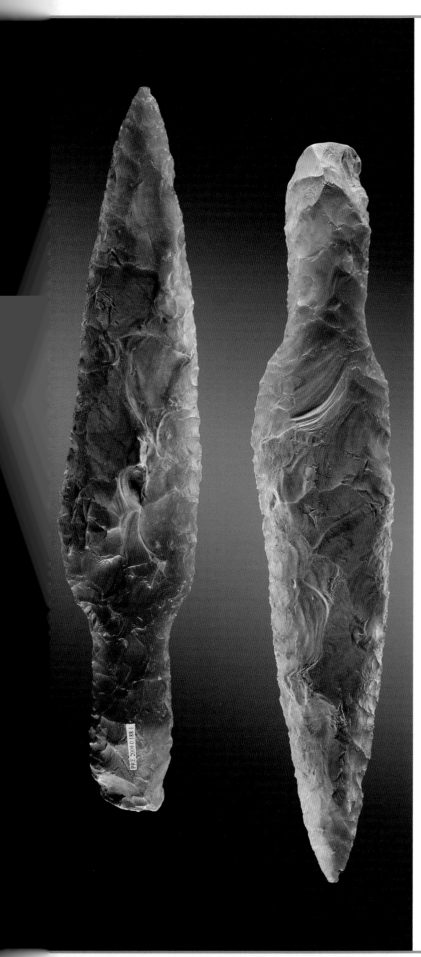

The Stone Age

The dagger began as a weapon of bone or stone. The human hand may be an extraordinarily adept tool for grasping and manipulating objects, but it is not nearly equal as a weapon to the tooth, claw, tusk, or horn of the wild animal, and human ingenuity applied itself very quickly to the task of equaling and surpassing such weapons. Over tens of thousands of years, the art of crafting stone blades was refined, in both the selection and the treatment of materials. At their finest, Stone Age knives are objects of remarkable beauty—and astonishingly sharp edges.

TWO VIEWS of a Neolithic dagger from c. 1800 BCE, displaying the skill and artistry of pressure flaking. This extraordinarily well-preserved dagger is both a keenly sharp weapon and a beautiful piece of functionalist design.

Paleolithic and Neolithic Knives

The earliest knife technologies involved stone, and Neolithic blade makers in particular developed an impressive array of skills for fashioning sharp and ergonomic blades. Flint, obsidian, and similar stones were sharpened by means of pressure flaking—not striking stone to stone (knapping) but applying precise amounts of pressure, using a suitable piece of bone or antler as a tool, to flake off the desired amount of material. Recent evidence suggests that, as early as 70,000 BCE, people in what is now South Africa were heat-treating local stones to alter their crystalline structure for more consistent, controllable flaking. Given that an undesired result of heat treatment was a more brittle edge, these early bladesmiths were already dealing with the variables that would challenge their successors over the ensuing millennia. While some stone blades were meant to fit snugly into the palm, others were fitted with handles of wood or other materials. Some, such as the Hindsgavl dagger, are objects of remarkable beauty.

Fine serrations on blade

Wooden handle fitted around base of blade

A close view showing where the blade inserts into a socket formed by two scales of wood sandwiched together.

GERMAN FLINT DAGGER

A well-preserved flint knife dating to 2900 BCE, found near Allensberg, Germany, where a Neolithic settlement was excavated by Lake Constance. The blade is, like all knapped stone blades, serrated, and the blade profile is suited to piercing as well as slicing. Note how the wooden handle has been preserved, revealing the practical mountings of such sharp stone blades.

Expert, even flaking of edge

THE HINDSGAVL DAGGER

The Hindsgavl Dagger, found in 1876 on the Danish island of Faenø. It represents the pinnacle of Neolithic blade manufacture during what has come to be called the Dagger Period, from approximately 2400–1800 BCE. Beautifully fashioned, it follows the "fishtail" form, so called because of its flared hilt in the shape of a fish's tailfin.

NORTHERN ITALIAN NEOLITHIC FLINT DAGGER

A flint blade from the Horgener Culture, which flourished around 3000 BCE in parts of Switzerland and Northern Italy. The finely formed blade has been fitted with a contemporary reproduction of the sort of handle used widely at the time, involving wooden plates bound around the base of the blade with cords.

Reproduction cord binding shows how the blade would have been affixed to a wooden handle

Leather binding

RECONSTRUCTED NEOLITHIC KNIFE

A contemporary replica of a Stone Age blade found in the mountains of Austria, mounted in a fashion appropriate to the time and place. The long, solid wood handle is fitted to the stone blade with leather cords wrapped around a crude, resin-based adhesive. An incision around the base of the handle could be used for attaching a wrist thong or decorative trim.

Extremely fine serrations

Egyptian Flint Weapons

In the modern Western imagination, ancient Egypt figures as a place of monumental pyramids and temples, priests and pharaohs, and opulent ornamentation. But the history of Egypt extends far back into prehistory, and some of the finest specimens of Neolithic work have been unearthed around the Nile. Many of these blades, including some curved daggers and the distinctive fishtail knife, are early versions of tools and weapons that enjoyed a long history of manufacture and use through millennia of Egyptian history. These early blades already show a distinctively Egyptian decorative sensibility, in the use of gold accents as well as ornamental patterns.

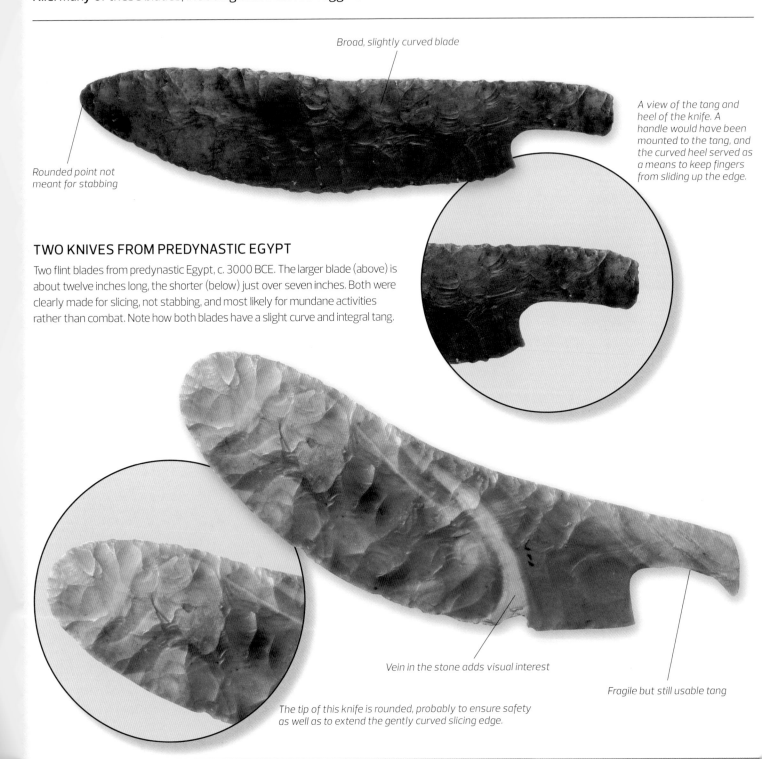

Broad, slightly curved blade

A view of the tang and heel of the knife. A handle would have been mounted to the tang, and the curved heel served as a means to keep fingers from sliding up the edge.

Rounded point not meant for stabbing

TWO KNIVES FROM PREDYNASTIC EGYPT

Two flint blades from predynastic Egypt, c. 3000 BCE. The larger blade (above) is about twelve inches long, the shorter (below) just over seven inches. Both were clearly made for slicing, not stabbing, and most likely for mundane activities rather than combat. Note how both blades have a slight curve and integral tang.

Vein in the stone adds visual interest

Fragile but still usable tang

The tip of this knife is rounded, probably to ensure safety as well as to extend the gently curved slicing edge.

EGYPTIAN FLINT KNIFE

An Egyptian flint knife from about 3,500 BCE. It anticipates later blades in its lack of a piercing point and its slight curve, indicating its primary role as a slicing rather than piercing tool. Also missing is an integrated tang, indicating that it was designed not to accept a handle mount but to fit snugly in the user's hand.

Straight spine to the blade

Rounded base of blade to fit in user's hand

Expertly curved and tapered point

The use of decorative gold overlay anticipates the opulence of future Egyptian decorative arts.

RIPPLE-FLAKED FLINT AND GOLD

An Egyptian blade from the Naqada II period, around 3000 BCE. This eight-inch blade is elegantly shaped, with an acute point suitable for piercing as well as slicing, and its butt end is coated in gold. Significantly, it is also single-edged—a development that prefigures the long history of gently curved, single-edged dagger blades of Egypt and the Middle East.

Cutting surface within notch

Tapered handle

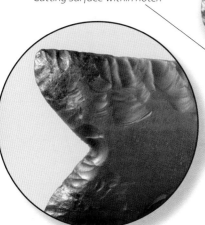

Handle still edged, though not sharp

A close view of the expertly sharpened, notched blade, which was almost certainly meant for ritual use. This blade form has been found in many Egyptian tombs.

EGYPTIAN FISHTAIL KNIFE

An Egyptian flint knife known as a "fishtail," but of a very different sort from those found in Northern Europe. The blade, just over six inches long, tapers steadily to a fairly acute point—but the real cutting surface is the v-shaped notch opposite the point. Since many of these blades have been unearthed in tombs, often in excellent condition, scholars believe the knives' primary use was in funerary rites or preparations.

Stone Axes

Next to knives, axes were the most important sharpened implements of the Stone Age. Both Paleolithic and Neolithic craftsmen appear to have made liberal use of chopping blades, both as tools and as weapons. The form of the blade depended partly on the stone from which it was made: flaking stones like flint were too brittle to stand up under hard use as high-impact tools, so harder stones were often painstakingly sharpened to serve as axe-heads. The problem was chiefly one of attaching the axe-head securely to a shaft. Since the materials from which such mountings would have been crafted have left few traces over the intervening millennia, archaeologists have had to rely on a combination of material evidence and informed speculation as to how axes would have been constructed.

STONE HAND-AXE

This Paleolithic hand-axe was discovered in gravel pits in southern England. Its near-heart shape reflects an advanced stone-working style.

A close view showing how precise pressure flaking could be. The almost rectangular flake was removed here; the pressure was directed straight across to the edge of the stone.

No fine serrations on grip

FLINT AXE

Uncovered in Denmark, this impressive example of a flint axe dates from around 10,000 BCE. By the time of this early Mesolithic (middle Stone Age) era, tools such as this were vital for the hunting activities that had become well established among the primitive peoples. Note the especially detailed chiseling on the axe edges.

Fine shaping of the blade's substantial cross-section

JADEITE AXE

This impressive Neolithic axe from 4,000–2,000 BCE was discovered in Canterbury, southern England. It was fashioned from jadeite, a material that was particularly challenging to work with due to its density.

Handle tapers to a point that could be used for some tasks

Smooth, easily grasped handle

GREENSTONE CELT

Archaeologists use the term celt (from the late Latin *celtis*, meaning "chisel") to describe the stone (and later bronze) axe- and adze-heads used by early peoples. These celts, from North America, are made from greenstone. A very hard rock found in riverbeds, greenstone is hard to work, but its durability is similar to that of iron. While these celts were used as woodworking tools, they and similar blades are the early ancestors of weapons like the battle-axe.

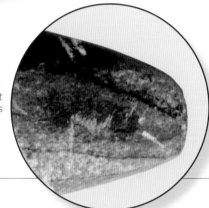

Because greenstone is found in riverbeds, it is rounded by erosion. As a result, edges take a great deal of work, but handles such as this one are naturally comfortable in the hand.

A close view of the groove in the head. Most likely, leather straps or cords would be wrapped around a forked wooden shaft here to secure the head.

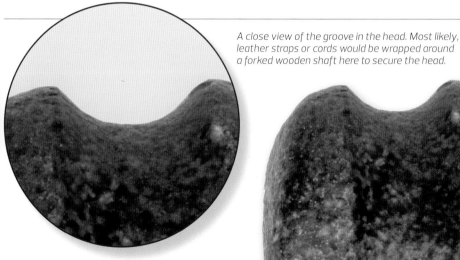

AXE-HEAD

A full-grooved axe-head dating from between 1000 and 1500 BCE. The groove allowed the head to be mounted on a wooden handle.

Ancient Blades

The Bronze Age

The problem with stone blades was that they broke easily and could not be restored. When smelting technology was developed in the early Bronze Age, first copper and then the most durable of copper alloys, bronze, became the material of choice for blades. Bronze is easily worked and resists corrosion. Its ability to be intricately shaped led to a variety of decorative techniques as well, such that the daggers of such cultures as Bactria, Luristan, China, Egypt, and Mycenae are often art objects as well as weapons. They also served ritual purposes.

Decorative design on hilt

Simple horse–head pommel

SHANG DYNASTY BRONZE KNIVES

Two very different Shang Dynasty knives, one with a broad blade and substantial hilt, and one with a slender blade and a tapered and figured hilt. The larger of the two knives (left), which might also have been mounted as a dagger–axe, has a single-edged blade with substantial heel and bolster, and a pistol–shaped hilt carved with geometric designs that may have been inlaid with turquoise. The smaller knife (right), also single-edged, has a gentle inward curve that continues into the hilt, with its horse–head pommel.

AN ANCIENT EGYPTIAN bas-relief showing captured prisoners. At the center of the image is a hieroglyph of a single-edged knife with a prominent heel and straight handle.

Chinese Bronze Knives

While stone blades were quite effective as both tools and weapons, they lacked two critical qualities: durability and reparability. A broken stone blade cannot be restored, and it was likely because of this consideration that early smiths had in mind when they turned their heat-treating skills to metal as well as stone. First copper and then copper alloys, most prominently bronze, served as the medium for knife blades. The dagger takes its most recognizable forms with Bronze Age craftsmanship. In what is now China, early smiths exploited the ability to cast bronze in representative shapes, incise it with ornamental patterns, and inlay it with precious materials.

SHANG DYNASTY FIGURED KNIVES

Two bronze knives from the Shang Dynasty (c.1600–1046 BCE). These weapons, which date from toward the dynasty's end, are both fitted with animal-head pommels—one of a ram and the other of a horse, both of which are decorated with turquoise inlay. The horse-head knife is better preserved, and reveals the ergonomic soundness of the design, in which the slight curve of the single-edged blade continues into the handle.

Pommel cast in the form of a ram's head

Horse-head pommel with turquoise inlay

Turquoise inlay on grip

NORTHERN CHINESE OR MONGOLIAN KNIFE

A slender cast bronze knife from northern China or perhaps Mongolia, c. 5th century BCE. The handle is incised with a zigzag pattern and a small pommel in the form of a hawk's head. The working blade, approximately four inches long, is single-edged and tapers to an acute stabbing point.

Hawk's head pommel

NORTHERN CHINESE KNIFE

A superb 5th-century BCE dagger from northern China, with an ornate openwork pommel and figured crossguard. The handle was likely wrapped, and the guard was probably inlaid with turquoise or other precious materials. The five-inch blade is nicely forged, with a raised center ridge and an even taper to a stabbing point.

Finely cast curve on openwork pommel

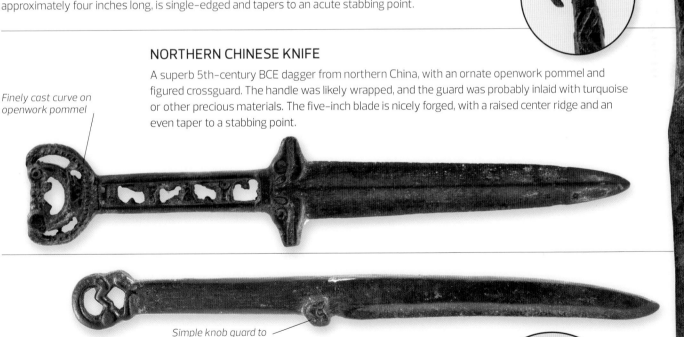

Simple knob guard to protect fingers

Small openwork pommel

SOUTHERN SIBERIAN KNIFE

A simple but effective bronze knife from Siberia or Mongolia, about the 5th century BCE. It has a small openwork pommel and a button-like guard at the base of its single-edged, five-inch blade. Like many such knives, it likely doubled as a utility knife and a self-defense weapon.

Narrow blade with gradual taper

Chinese Bronze Axes

Just as the stone knife gave way to the bronze dagger, so did the stone axe-head lead to the bronze battle-axe. In ancient China, axe blades in a variety of shapes found use as weapons, tools, and ritual objects. One weapon that gained particular prominence was the dagger-axe, a kind of pole arm with a head that often combines a straight, double-edged dagger blade with an angled, sickle-like shearing edge. During the Qin Dynasty (221–206 BCE), millions of these weapons were produced for military campaigns that ranged across thousands of miles of contested territory. Dagger-axes became so prominent that ritual blades of jade were also produced, to be found thousands of years later in period tombs.

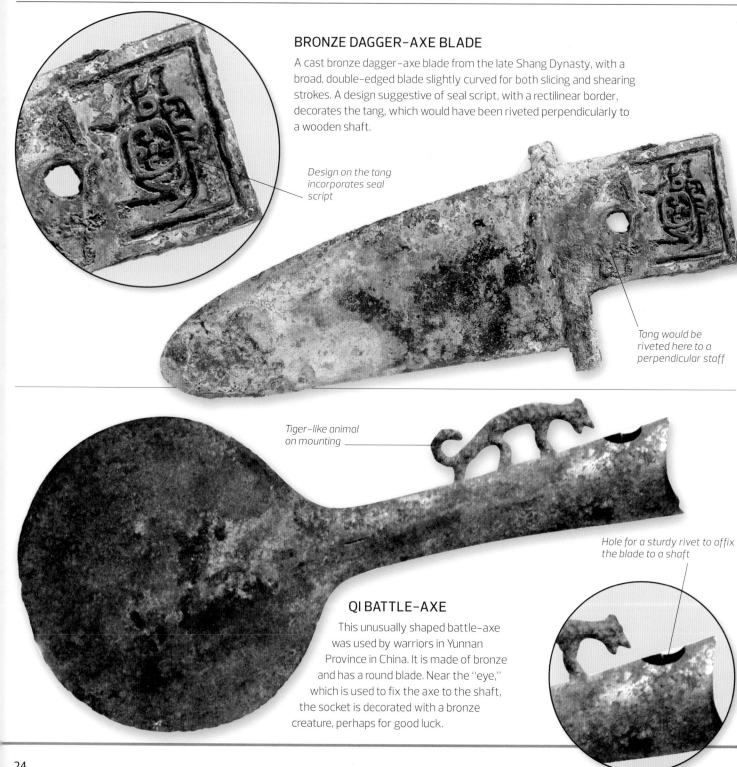

BRONZE DAGGER-AXE BLADE

A cast bronze dagger-axe blade from the late Shang Dynasty, with a broad, double-edged blade slightly curved for both slicing and shearing strokes. A design suggestive of seal script, with a rectilinear border, decorates the tang, which would have been riveted perpendicularly to a wooden shaft.

Design on the tang incorporates seal script

Tang would be riveted here to a perpendicular staff

Tiger-like animal on mounting

Hole for a sturdy rivet to affix the blade to a shaft

QI BATTLE-AXE

This unusually shaped battle-axe was used by warriors in Yunnan Province in China. It is made of bronze and has a round blade. Near the "eye," which is used to fix the axe to the shaft, the socket is decorated with a bronze creature, perhaps for good luck.

Precisely drilled rivets for mounting to a wooden or bronze shaft

OPENWORK DAGGER-AXE BLADE

A cast bronze dagger-axe blade from the late Shang Dynasty. It features openwork construction, with decorative designs reminiscent of seal script as well as images of masks, a cicada, and a bird. Most likely, this was a ritual or symbolic item, as the openwork casting was not sufficiently durable for battlefield use, and the decorative work suggests it was intended chiefly for display.

Geometric designs on openwork ribs

CHINESE JADE CEREMONIAL DAGGER-AXE BLADE

A polished jade dagger-axe blade from the Shang Dynasty (c. 1600–1050 BCE). With its double fuller, chisel-like point, and rivet holes, this is a strikingly realistic blade meant purely for symbolic or ritual use. It may be that on occasion shafts were riveted to jade blades, but we have no evidence of this. More likely, this was a symbol of authority, or a ritual implement meant to protect against enemies.

Stylized case image of a bird

Southeast Asian Bronze Knives

During the Bronze Age, several cultures in Southeast Asia, especially what is now Vietnam, brought tremendous refinement to bronze metalwork. The Dong Son culture, which lived in the river valleys of northern Vietnam, became famed for casting in bronze; Dong Son drums were exported all over East Asia, and they also produced impressive figurines. Dong Son daggers often incorporate cast figures into their designs, usually at the pommel. The Sa Huynh culture, which flourished to the south of the Dong Son, practiced many of the same casting techniques and used similar decorative motifs.

FIGURED DONG SON DAGGER

A bronze dagger of the Dong Son culture, from approximately 400 BCE. The entire handle is cast in the form of a human being, possibly wearing regalia of some sort. It may be that the dagger was used for ritual purposes. The broad, double-edged blade, about six inches long, tapers to a fairly acute point, its edges narrowing in a gentle curve toward the tip.

Carefully cast figure of a boar or elephant

Handle flares at base into a simple guard

Traditional headdress on figure

Large earrings, probably of cast bronze in real life

Small holes cast in the guard

BRONZE DAGGER, SA HUYNH CULTURE

A bronze dagger of the Sa Huynh culture, which flourished to the south of the Dong Son in the same time period. Though the Sa Huynh were skilled at working with iron, many bronze artifacts have also been unearthed in central and southern Vietnam. This dagger has a nicely flared handle and a pommel in the shape of an animal—either a boar or an elephant. Note how the small holes cast in the guard resemble those in Dong Son knives.

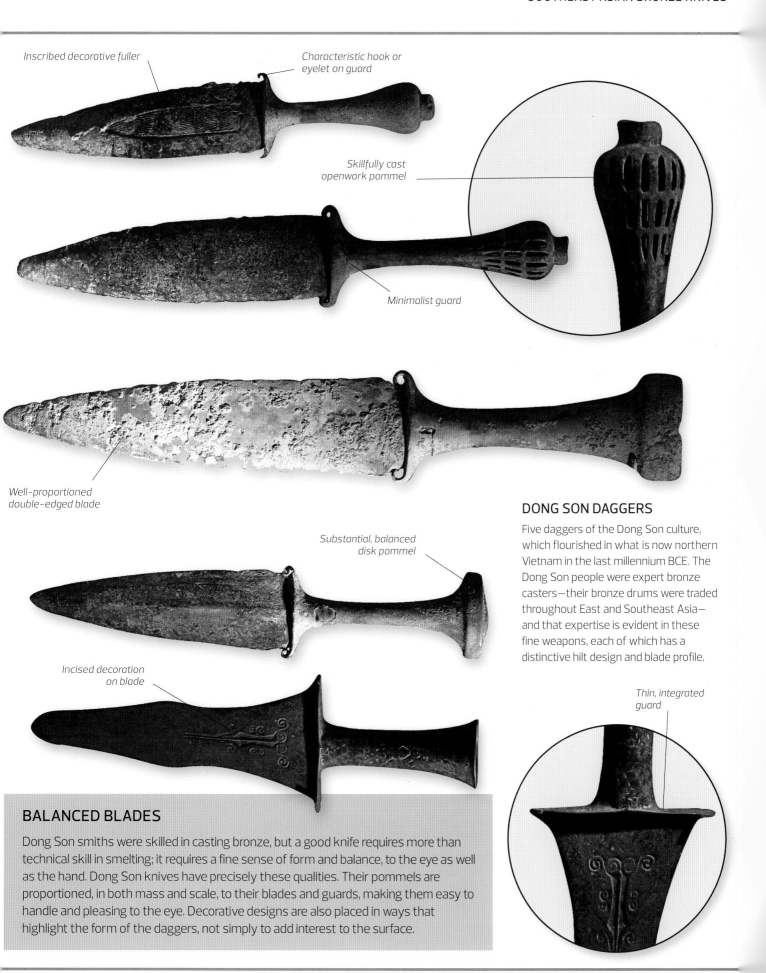

Inscribed decorative fuller

Characteristic hook or eyelet on guard

Skillfully cast openwork pommel

Minimalist guard

Well-proportioned double-edged blade

Substantial, balanced disk pommel

Incised decoration on blade

Thin, integrated guard

DONG SON DAGGERS

Five daggers of the Dong Son culture, which flourished in what is now northern Vietnam in the last millennium BCE. The Dong Son people were expert bronze casters—their bronze drums were traded throughout East and Southeast Asia—and that expertise is evident in these fine weapons, each of which has a distinctive hilt design and blade profile.

BALANCED BLADES

Dong Son smiths were skilled in casting bronze, but a good knife requires more than technical skill in smelting; it requires a fine sense of form and balance, to the eye as well as the hand. Dong Son knives have precisely these qualities. Their pommels are proportioned, in both mass and scale, to their blades and guards, making them easy to handle and pleasing to the eye. Decorative designs are also placed in ways that highlight the form of the daggers, not simply to add interest to the surface.

Central Asian and Turkish Bronze Age Knives

It is easy to think of Bronze Age civilizations as being for the most part isolated within their own histories and those of their immediate neighbors, but the era saw the rise and fall of vast empires and the beginnings of the trade ties that would form the Silk Road. From China to Turkey and even beyond, goods passed through trade and conquest, and with them went weapon-making technologies. Daggers and other knives from throughout Central Asia and into the Middle East often share elements of design and decoration—but different cultures also preferred different blade profiles. In many cases, these blades clearly served more than one purpose, being both practical tools and weapons for self-defense or even war.

Hilt forms an insert for the iron tang

Hilt constructed to accommodate scales for the grip

Acute iron blade tip

Rivets and bars remain from the sheath

IRON AND GOLD BRONZE AGE DAGGER, TURKEY

Though this dagger, found in Turkey, dates to the Bronze Age, its blade is actually iron, and its mountings of gold. Its stylish hilt ends in a wide pommel of curved "horns," almost as wide as the blade itself is long. The gold-plated grip is riveted to the tang, and at the midpoint of the blade is the gold trim from what was once the dagger's sheath.

FORGING A BRONZE BLADE

Bronze melts at a relatively low temperature compared to other malleable metals, and is easily worked. During the Bronze Age, most blades were produced from molds of either stone or clay; the clay molds were probably formed using existing knives or swords. Once the two halves of the mold were prepared, they had to be fitted together and heated sufficiently that, when molten bronze was poured in one end, it would remain liquid all the way to the other. When the bronze set, the mold was removed—clay molds would probably break at this point—and the blade and tang would be hammered into shape, sharpened, and polished. Only then would it be riveted to a hilt.

Etched lines at transition from blade to handle

Cast cow's head pommel

MINIMALIST CENTRAL ASIAN DAGGER

A simple cast bronze knife from Central Asia, c. 5th century BCE. The handle extends without interruption from the blade, and ends in a cow's head pommel. There is also some etched decoration. The four-inch blade is single-edged, and most likely made to be more of a tool than a weapon.

CENTRAL ASIAN DAGGER WITH CHINESE INFLUENCE

A Central Asian cast bronze dagger from c. 1100 BCE. Its ten-inch blade is double-edged and tapers continuously to an acute stabbing point; a central ridge serves to strengthen the blade. The hilt is decidedly Chinese in style, with a fine, decoratively incised guard and a figured pommel. The grip would have been wrapped in cord and/or fabric and leather.

Figured cast pommel

Central ridge on blade

Chinese-style guard and bolster

CYPRIOT BLADE

A bronze blade from Cyprus, c. 3000–2400 BCE. Cyprus was home to Bronze Age settlers long before the Greeks and other peoples of the region began to settle it. This blade, which resembles that of a long spearhead, has a raised central ridge and is clearly designed for thrusting attacks in combat. Its slender tang would have been fitted to a substantial grip.

Acute blade with diamond cross-section

Bronze Blades of Luristan

Luristan (also spelled Lorestan) is a mountainous region in the west of what is now Iran, but during the Bronze Age it was home to one of the most sophisticated metalworking traditions of its time. The bronze sculptures and weapons of Luristan are remarkable for their variety as much as their workmanship. Only in the late 1920s, when the European market was suddenly flooded with Luristan bronzes clearly looted from tombs and other sites, did the full extent of the region's metalworking tradition become apparent to Western scholars and collectors. Apart from its metalwork, most of the culture of Bronze Age Luristan remains a mystery; even the ethnicity of the people who produced these impressive daggers is uncertain. What we do know is that they manufactured some of the finest blades of the Bronze Age.

BRONZE LURISTAN DAGGER

A fine example of a Luristan bronze dagger from approximately 750 BCE. This well-proportioned weapon has a double-edged blade with a raised center ridge and an acute stabbing point. A sturdy bolster connects with a handle grooved for better grip when wrapped, and a button-shaped pommel. The cast hilt is hollow, and could have been inlaid with a range of materials.

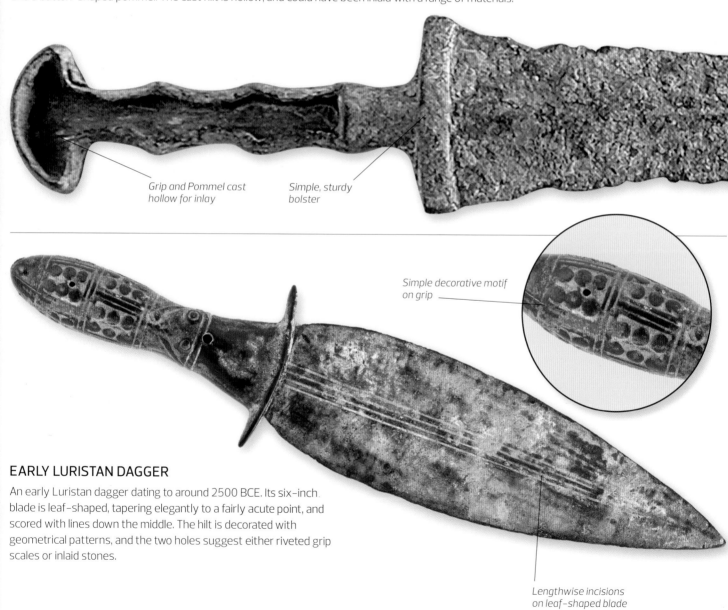

Grip and Pommel cast hollow for inlay

Simple, sturdy bolster

Simple decorative motif on grip

EARLY LURISTAN DAGGER

An early Luristan dagger dating to around 2500 BCE. Its six-inch blade is leaf-shaped, tapering elegantly to a fairly acute point, and scored with lines down the middle. The hilt is decorated with geometrical patterns, and the two holes suggest either riveted grip scales or inlaid stones.

Lengthwise incisions on leaf-shaped blade

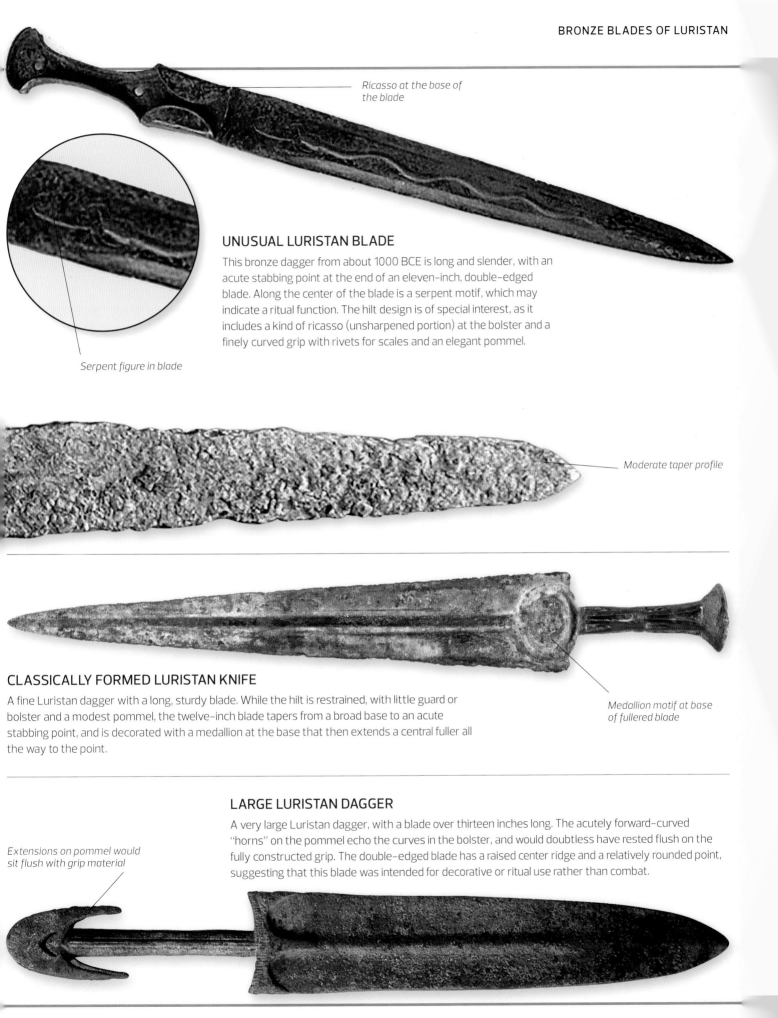

Ricasso at the base of the blade

Serpent figure in blade

UNUSUAL LURISTAN BLADE

This bronze dagger from about 1000 BCE is long and slender, with an acute stabbing point at the end of an eleven-inch, double-edged blade. Along the center of the blade is a serpent motif, which may indicate a ritual function. The hilt design is of special interest, as it includes a kind of ricasso (unsharpened portion) at the bolster and a finely curved grip with rivets for scales and an elegant pommel.

Moderate taper profile

CLASSICALLY FORMED LURISTAN KNIFE

A fine Luristan dagger with a long, sturdy blade. While the hilt is restrained, with little guard or bolster and a modest pommel, the twelve-inch blade tapers from a broad base to an acute stabbing point, and is decorated with a medallion at the base that then extends a central fuller all the way to the point.

Medallion motif at base of fullered blade

LARGE LURISTAN DAGGER

A very large Luristan dagger, with a blade over thirteen inches long. The acutely forward-curved "horns" on the pommel echo the curves in the bolster, and would doubtless have rested flush on the fully constructed grip. The double-edged blade has a raised center ridge and a relatively rounded point, suggesting that this blade was intended for decorative or ritual use rather than combat.

Extensions on pommel would sit flush with grip material

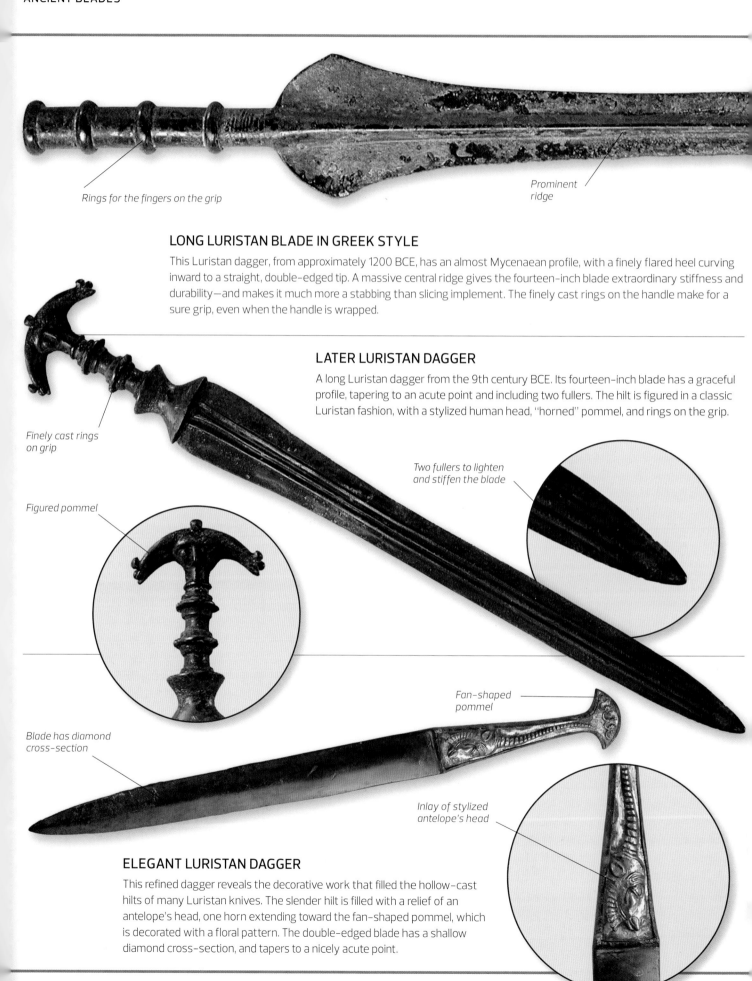

Rings for the fingers on the grip

Prominent ridge

LONG LURISTAN BLADE IN GREEK STYLE

This Luristan dagger, from approximately 1200 BCE, has an almost Mycenaean profile, with a finely flared heel curving inward to a straight, double-edged tip. A massive central ridge gives the fourteen-inch blade extraordinary stiffness and durability—and makes it much more a stabbing than slicing implement. The finely cast rings on the handle make for a sure grip, even when the handle is wrapped.

LATER LURISTAN DAGGER

A long Luristan dagger from the 9th century BCE. Its fourteen-inch blade has a graceful profile, tapering to an acute point and including two fullers. The hilt is figured in a classic Luristan fashion, with a stylized human head, "horned" pommel, and rings on the grip.

Finely cast rings on grip

Two fullers to lighten and stiffen the blade

Figured pommel

Blade has diamond cross-section

Fan-shaped pommel

Inlay of stylized antelope's head

ELEGANT LURISTAN DAGGER

This refined dagger reveals the decorative work that filled the hollow-cast hilts of many Luristan knives. The slender hilt is filled with a relief of an antelope's head, one horn extending toward the fan-shaped pommel, which is decorated with a floral pattern. The double-edged blade has a shallow diamond cross-section, and tapers to a nicely acute point.

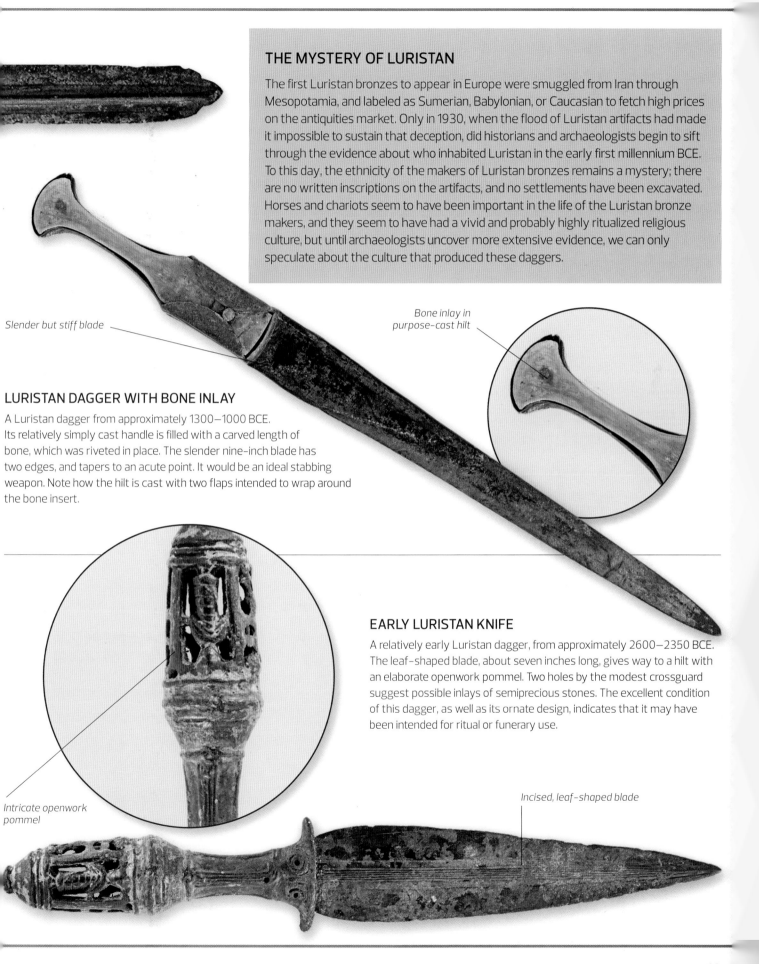

THE MYSTERY OF LURISTAN

The first Luristan bronzes to appear in Europe were smuggled from Iran through Mesopotamia, and labeled as Sumerian, Babylonian, or Caucasian to fetch high prices on the antiquities market. Only in 1930, when the flood of Luristan artifacts had made it impossible to sustain that deception, did historians and archaeologists begin to sift through the evidence about who inhabited Luristan in the early first millennium BCE. To this day, the ethnicity of the makers of Luristan bronzes remains a mystery; there are no written inscriptions on the artifacts, and no settlements have been excavated. Horses and chariots seem to have been important in the life of the Luristan bronze makers, and they seem to have had a vivid and probably highly ritualized religious culture, but until archaeologists uncover more extensive evidence, we can only speculate about the culture that produced these daggers.

Slender but stiff blade

Bone inlay in purpose-cast hilt

LURISTAN DAGGER WITH BONE INLAY

A Luristan dagger from approximately 1300–1000 BCE. Its relatively simply cast handle is filled with a carved length of bone, which was riveted in place. The slender nine-inch blade has two edges, and tapers to an acute point. It would be an ideal stabbing weapon. Note how the hilt is cast with two flaps intended to wrap around the bone insert.

EARLY LURISTAN KNIFE

A relatively early Luristan dagger, from approximately 2600–2350 BCE. The leaf-shaped blade, about seven inches long, gives way to a hilt with an elaborate openwork pommel. Two holes by the modest crossguard suggest possible inlays of semiprecious stones. The excellent condition of this dagger, as well as its ornate design, indicates that it may have been intended for ritual or funerary use.

Intricate openwork pommel

Incised, leaf-shaped blade

Bronze Blades of Ancient Egypt

The most glorious centuries of ancient Egypt—the Old, Middle, and New Kingdoms—all unfolded during the Bronze Age, and the knives of the era served as both weapons and symbolic possessions indicating rank and wealth. A great variety of blade profiles characterize the knives of Bronze Age Egypt, from straight double-edged blades to broad and curved single-edged blades that were more likely utility or symbolic knives. Many blades were incised or impressed with hieroglyphic cartouches indicating the names and even the station of their owners.

EGYPTIAN DAGGER

A dagger belonging to a seal bearer from the 12th or 13th dynasty (1991–166 BCE). Seal bearers were direct representatives of the Pharaoh, and commanded tremendous power and prestige. This knife, incised with a hieroglyphic inscription, was doubtless one of many possessions that indicated the exalted status of its owner. The double-edged blade was probably seldom used, and certainly not meant for combat.

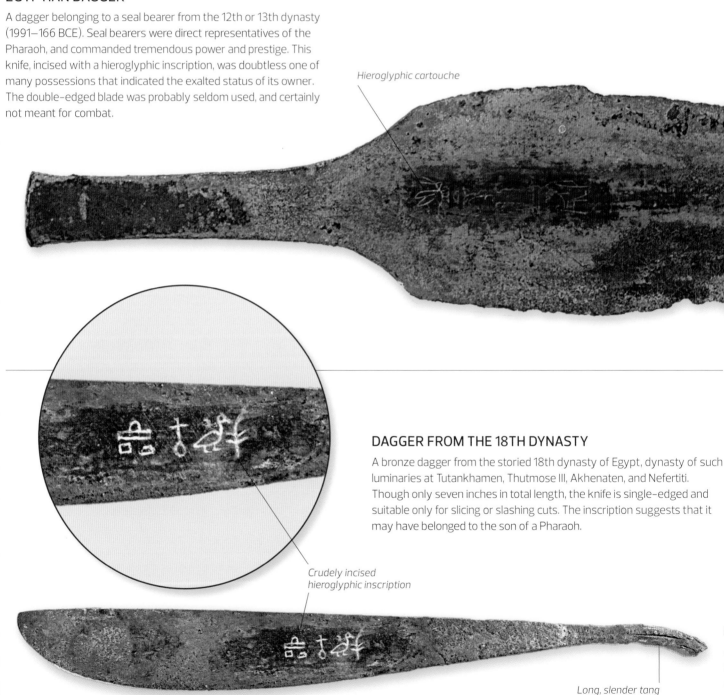

Hieroglyphic cartouche

DAGGER FROM THE 18TH DYNASTY

A bronze dagger from the storied 18th dynasty of Egypt, dynasty of such luminaries at Tutankhamen, Thutmose III, Akhenaten, and Nefertiti. Though only seven inches in total length, the knife is single-edged and suitable only for slicing or slashing cuts. The inscription suggests that it may have belonged to the son of a Pharaoh.

Crudely incised hieroglyphic inscription

Long, slender tang

Hieroglyphics identifying the owner

Broad, rounded blade profile

EGYPTIAN PRINCE'S DAGGER

A bronze dagger owned by Wadj-Mose, a prince of the 18th dynasty. The broad, two-edged blade tapers to a somewhat rounded point, though deterioration over the millennia may have altered its profile. It is incised with hieroglyphics indicating its ownership. The hilt features a concave grip flaring to a modest, disk-shaped pommel.

Moderate taper profile

Hieroglyphic cartouche

Some degradation to the hilt

DAGGER HILT FROM THE 19TH DYNASTY

An ornate dagger hilt from about the reign of the great Pharaoh Ramses II (1304–1237 BCE), considered by many scholars to be the Pharaoh of the Book of Exodus. The handle contains a prominent and elaborate hieroglyphic cartouche, and widens to accommodate the base of a substantial blade, now lost.

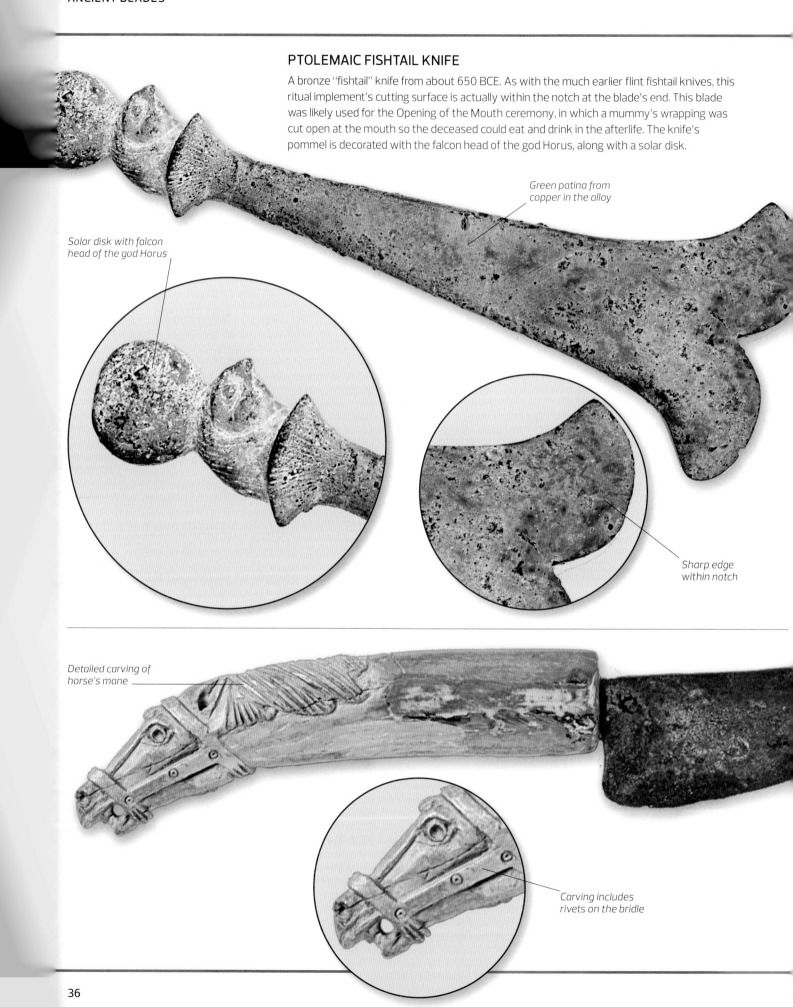

PTOLEMAIC FISHTAIL KNIFE

A bronze "fishtail" knife from about 650 BCE. As with the much earlier flint fishtail knives, this ritual implement's cutting surface is actually within the notch at the blade's end. This blade was likely used for the Opening of the Mouth ceremony, in which a mummy's wrapping was cut open at the mouth so the deceased could eat and drink in the afterlife. The knife's pommel is decorated with the falcon head of the god Horus, along with a solar disk.

Green patina from copper in the alloy

Solar disk with falcon head of the god Horus

Sharp edge within notch

Detailed carving of horse's mane

Carving includes rivets on the bridle

A RITUAL KNIFE?

The fishtail knives of ancient Egypt have posed an abiding mystery to archaeologists and historians. What would be the purpose of these notch-bladed knives, especially since they occur in large numbers in Egyptian tombs across the millennia? A consensus eventually formed that fishtail knives likely played a role in the Opening of the Mouth Ceremony, in which a mummy's wrapping was ritually sliced open at the mouth to allow the dead to ingest food in the afterlife. Some scholars doubt this interpretation, not least because flint fishtail knives predate the ritualized process of mummification. It may be that fishtail knives served as a badge of rank, and continued in that symbolic function into the Ptolemaic era.

Pommel may have been cast in the shape of a crocodile's head

HELLENISTIC EGYPTIAN DAGGER

A bronze dagger from the Hellenistic period (c. 300 BCE–300 CE). This slender knife includes a turned handle, elegantly designed to afford a sure grip, and ending in an extended pommel. The blade, about four inches long, is double-edged and rounded at the point, indicating that the knife was for practical or ritual use rather than combat.

Double-edged, slightly rounded blade

Scalloped bolster at the base of the blade

Slender, gently recurved blade

ROMAN EGYPTIAN KNIFE

A fascinating dagger from the Romanized period of Egyptian history, during the 1st and 2nd centuries CE. The elaborate ivory handle, carved to resemble a bridled horse, is fitted to a four-inch recurved blade that anticipates the khanjar daggers of later centuries. This is a fine piece of workmanship; note the detailed rendering of the horse's mane.

Greek and Roman Knives

The great civilizations of Greece, from the early Minoans to the city-states of the Classical period, had great traditions of weaponry. Though the primary combat weapon of ancient Greece was the spear, archaeological evidence reveals that daggers were also common, and often used to showcase sometimes strikingly beautiful decorative work. In ancient Rome, the dagger was even more prominent in both civilian and military life. Roman senators and other patricians often wore ornate daggers, and of course daggers figured in many of the assassinations that colored Roman imperial history.

BRONZE KNIFE FROM SANTORINI
Another ancient Greek dagger, in this case possibly Minoan. It comes from excavations at Santorini. It reveals the same blade profile and three-rivet hilt attachment as many other examples, and its decorative inlay has been largely lost over the millennia.

MYCENAEAN BRONZE KNIFE
A fine Mycenaean dagger unearthed at the Prosymna site near Corinth in southern Greece. The large rivets would have been used to attach the hilt; they almost obscure the exquisite decorative detail of a dolphin, inlaid in the middle of the blade. The blade itself is two-edged and reasonably acute.

Decorative inlay of a dolphin

Abruptly tapered blade tip

DETAIL OF MYCENAEAN KNIFE
A remarkable decorative scene from a Mycenaean dagger blade of the 16th century BCE. Inlaid with gold, it depicts hunters taking on an enraged lion, who has already slain one of the hunting party. Three of the remaining hunters use spears—the primary weapon of ancient Greece—but one is armed with a bow and arrows. The lion is beautifully rendered.

Vibrant inlay of an attacking lion

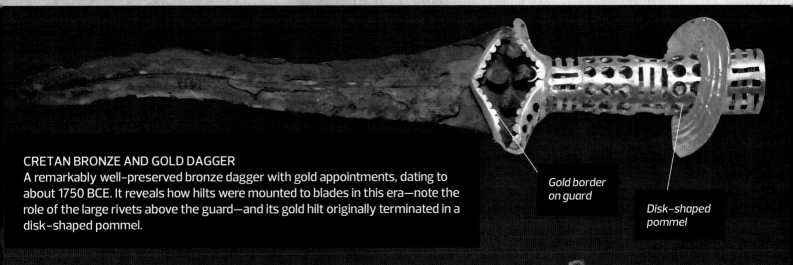

CRETAN BRONZE AND GOLD DAGGER

A remarkably well-preserved bronze dagger with gold appointments, dating to about 1750 BCE. It reveals how hilts were mounted to blades in this era—note the role of the large rivets above the guard—and its gold hilt originally terminated in a disk-shaped pommel.

Gold border on guard

Disk-shaped pommel

ROMAN DAGGER

A Roman military dagger, or *pugio*, dating from the Imperial period and unearthed at Oberstimm in Germany. This impressive weapon is a smaller version of a *gladius*, or Roman short sword. The blade is most suitable for stabbing, but can also be used for slashing. The cruciform guard and balanced pommel set the pattern for the arming swords of Medieval Europe.

Rivet holes for grip scales

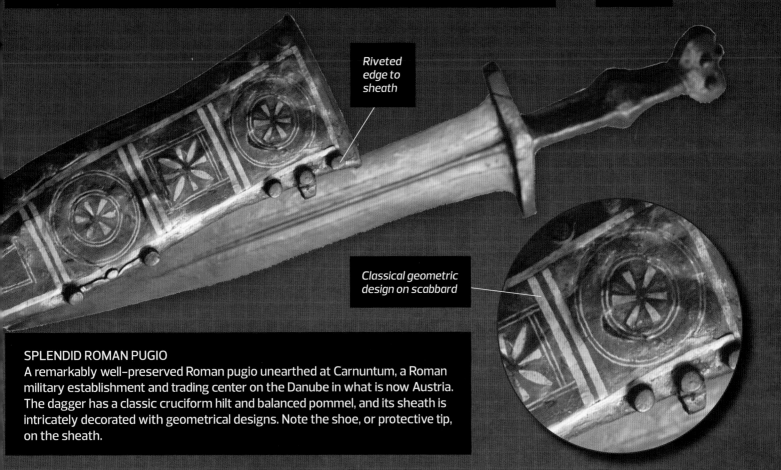

Riveted edge to sheath

Classical geometric design on scabbard

SPLENDID ROMAN PUGIO

A remarkably well-preserved Roman pugio unearthed at Carnuntum, a Roman military establishment and trading center on the Danube in what is now Austria. The dagger has a classic cruciform hilt and balanced pommel, and its sheath is intricately decorated with geometrical designs. Note the shoe, or protective tip, on the sheath.

Bronze Age Knives of Europe

Europe outside the Classical world had its own traditions of knifemaking, many of them Celtic in origin, and during the Bronze Age they gained remarkable sophistication of both manufacture and decoration. The Hallstatt Culture, named after the location of a burial site discovered in Austria, dominated Central Europe in the first half of the first millennium BCE before being succeeded by the Iron Age La Tène culture. Both made magnificent knives, many in the style known as "antenna weapons," named for the antenna-like decorative arms extending from their pommels. The decorative work on such blades is superb, and European Bronze Age knives often have exceptional gold adornment as well. Even after the advent of iron and steel blades, bronze remained the preferred material for decorative elements.

Flare in tang for secure grip

IBERIAN DAGGER

An iron dagger from Iberia, c. 450–200 BCE, unearthed in what is now Andalusia. In form, the blade follows classic Roman design, with a broad base that tapers to an acute tip. The hilt includes a sturdy bolster and a winged pommel suggestive of the antenna swords and knives of some Celtic cultures.

BRONZE AGE CELTIC DAGGER

A bronze dagger unearthed at Sion in Switzerland, a major center of Celtic culture. Its balanced hilt, in which the curved bolster mirrors the curves of the pommel, is of the variety known as antenna swords, because of the resemblance of the pommel to antennae. The double-edged blade tapers to an effective stabbing point.

The blade's wide base fits securely into the curved guard

Classic antenna hilt

Intricately cast hilt

CELTIC BRONZE DISPLAY KNIFE

Of unknown date, this dagger is thought to have been used for display purposes, and may be Celtic in origin.

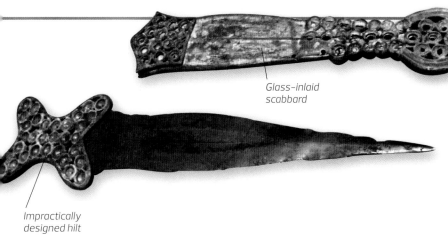

Glass-inlaid scabbard

Impractically designed hilt

COOKHAM BRONZE DAGGER, ENGLAND

The Cookham dagger, take from the Thames River near Cookham in England. This extraordinarily stylized and richly decorated knife remains one of the curiosities of Iron Age Britain. The blade is extremely acute but not likely for more than ritual use, as the ornate and less-than-ergonomic handle suggests. Both the scabbard and the hilt were inlaid with glass.

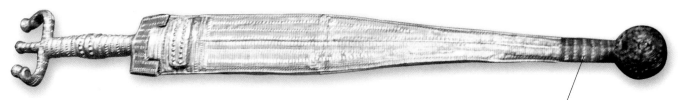

Carved reinforcement at tip of scabbard

THE HOCHDORF DAGGER

One of the most fascinating finds in European archaeology is the Hochdorf tomb, which dates to about 530 BCE. Its occupant, known as "the Tutankhamun of the Celts," was clearly a Celtic chieftain. Interred with him was this ornate dagger, shown here in its original bronze and iron form and with the intricate gold foil with which it was meticulously coated before being entombed with its owner. The dagger itself is a superb example of Celtic workmanship, with an acute iron blade and a finely cast antenna-style hilt.

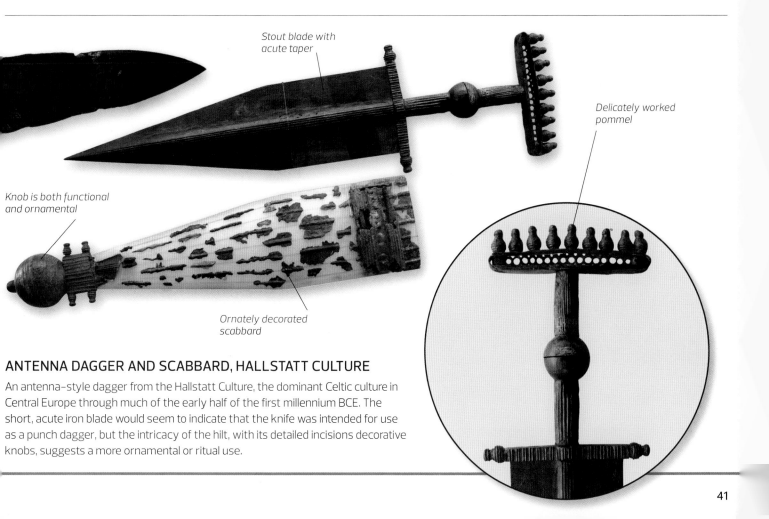

Stout blade with acute taper

Delicately worked pommel

Knob is both functional and ornamental

Ornately decorated scabbard

ANTENNA DAGGER AND SCABBARD, HALLSTATT CULTURE

An antenna-style dagger from the Hallstatt Culture, the dominant Celtic culture in Central Europe through much of the early half of the first millennium BCE. The short, acute iron blade would seem to indicate that the knife was intended for use as a punch dagger, but the intricacy of the hilt, with its detailed incisions decorative knobs, suggests a more ornamental or ritual use.

Bronze Age Axe-Heads and Clubs

The Bronze Age was a huge technological advance for humankind. During this period, people first learned how to create tools—and weapons—by refining, smelting, and casting metal ores. Because different cultures developed metalwork at different times, the term "Bronze Age" covers a wide time period. It is also something of a misnomer, because in its earliest phase, copper rather than true bronze (an alloy of about 90 percent copper and 10 percent tin) was used. This period is sometimes sub-categorized as the Chalcolithic Age. Copper metallurgy was known in China and the Eastern Mediterranean by 3500–3000 BCE, and over the next millennium or so the use of copper and, later, bronze spread into Europe and also developed independently in South America.

Once metalsmiths had figured out how to achieve the high temperatures needed to smelt iron ore by using charcoal, and how to fortify iron implements by hammering and tempering them in water, iron weapons began to replace those of copper and bronze. Historians generally date the start of the Iron Age to between 1200 and 1000 BCE. Around a thousand years later, Indian and Chinese metalsmiths learned how to combine iron with carbon to create an even stronger metal: steel.

Narrow blade profile, probably for close utility work

Flared blade

AXE-HEADS

A pair of Bronze Age copper axe-heads. Such an axe was carried by "Ötzi"—a mummified man whose remains, dating from about 3300 BCE, were found frozen into a glacier on the Austrian-Italian border in 1991. One theory about Ötzi's death holds that he died of wounds sustained from an attack by a band of hunters attempting to take his prized implement.

Carved "shoe" for fitting blade to shaft

ANCIENT EGYPTIAN COPPER BATTLE-AXE

This battle-axe has a long socket for the handle. The design is typical, with holes in the blade to make it lighter and save on precious raw materials.

Minimalist blade to preserve alloy

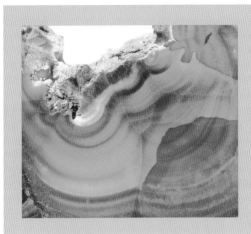

MAKING BRONZE

Key to the inception of metal weapons was the discovery of the means to extract a metal from its ore. In terms of bronze, a copper ore was heated in a charcoal fire and tin ore later added, to create a strong, adaptable alloy.

MOLDING THE MATERIAL

This mold (far left) was discovered near to a section of copper axe (near left) in Cát Tiên, southern Vietnam. The site was home to a civilization that dated from the 4th century CE, highlighting how copper was introduced across the world at different times.

Axe-head mold in sandy stone

Rough cast of a copper axe-head

Cast eyelet for affixing blade to shaft

Carved-out "shoe" for mounting the shaft

BRONZE AGE AXE-HEAD

This impressive bronze axe-head was among a number of 9th–8th-century BCE items found at St Erth in Cornwall, southwest England. Measuring 5 inches (13cm), the piece would have been cast in a mold and attached to a wooden handle.

he Medieval and Renaissance Dagger

The Dagger's Renaissance

In the early Middle Ages, the dagger had little use on a battlefield teeming with long swords, axes, arrows, and various kinds of armor; it remained, so history tells us, a civilian weapon, seldom valued or preserved. By the 13th century, however, with advances in armor and increased mercantile wealth, the dagger made a resounding comeback. Such late medieval and Renaissance daggers as the rondel, the sword-hilt dagger, the cinquedea, and the baselard became fixtures of male dress, serving as both weapons and displays of wealth and personal style. These classic daggers became the standard forms according to which future daggers would be designed.

A CLOSE VIEW of *The Ambassadors* by Hans Holbein the Younger, from 1533, showing an ornate dagger with a rondel-style pommel in the hand of what is most likely the French ambassador to the Court of Henry VIII.

Medieval European Daggers

The dagger did not feature prominently in medieval warfare, not least because it stood little chance of penetrating the increasingly formidable armor that developed over the course of the Middle Ages. But knives did play significant roles in civilian and civic life; magnificent daggers were worn as emblems of wealth and status, and in the streets of medieval cities, men carried several kinds of daggers for self-defense or less savory purposes. The main types of medieval European dagger were the sword hilt (or cruciform) dagger, which was patterned after an arming sword; the ballock knife, with a guard consisting of two round protrusions that gave the weapon its name; the rondel, with a disk-shaped guard and pommel; and the baselard, with an exceptionally long and stiff blade.

The pommel recalls the wheel pommels of medieval arming swords

The textured grip of the rondel, along with the disk-shaped guard and pommel, make for secure handling

The distinctive guard

Stiff blade with triangular cross-section

MODERN REPRODUCTIONS OF THREE MEDIEVAL DAGGERS

Modern reproductions of three common varieties of late medieval dagger. On the bottom is a ballock knife, so named because of its anatomically suggestive hilt. In the middle is a rondel dagger, known for its disk-shaped guard and pommel. On the top is a classic sword-hilt, or cruciform, dagger—essentially a miniature arming sword, in this case with a wheel pommel.

KAMPHUES DAGGER

An ornate dagger that is said to have belonged to Kort Kamphues, a famously corrupt judge and brigand (a striking combination) in 16th-century Westphalia in Germany. The dagger was made in the early 14th century for a nearby nobleman. Its hilt and parts of its elaborate sheath are of carved ivory, fitted with silver mountings. It is a superb example of an aristocratic medieval sidearm.

The scabbard is adorned with the coat of arms of the lords of Graes, a city near where the knife was made

Spiked scabbard tip

Intricately carved ivory hilt

BELGIAN BALLOCK KNIFE

This classic ballock knife—its name evident in the shape of its hilt—was uncovered in the Ten Duinen Cistercian Monastery in Belgium. The ballock knife was a mainstay of medieval European street fighting, especially in England; it was light, inexpensive, easily concealed, and fitted with a lethally acute, stiletto-like thrusting blade.

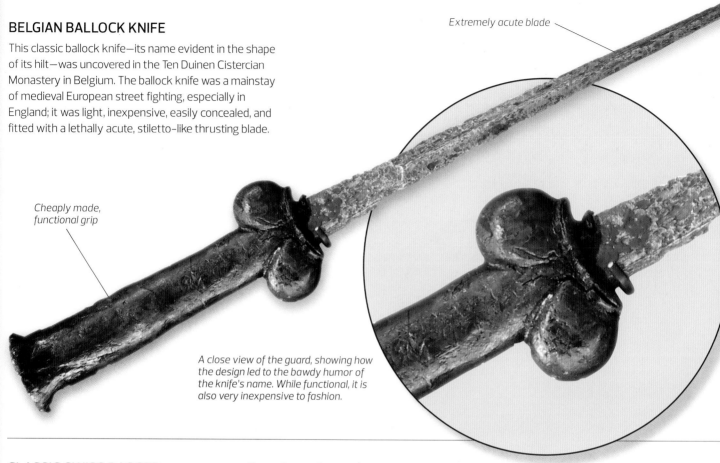

Extremely acute blade

Cheaply made, functional grip

A close view of the guard, showing how the design led to the bawdy humor of the knife's name. While functional, it is also very inexpensive to fashion.

CLASSIC SWISS DAGGER

A 14th-century Swiss dagger. Its forward-curved pommel and guard are in the style of a baselard, and its two-edged blade, reinforced with a raised center ridge, tapers to an effective if not especially acute stabbing point. Swiss daggers of this variety set the standard in Europe through much of the Middle Ages and the Renaissance.

Forward-curved pommel

Sturdy guard

Acute, double-edged blade

RONDEL DAGGER

A 15th-century Burgundian rondel dagger, possibly owned by the Holy Roman Emperor Maximilian I. The hand would fit securely between the round guard and pommel, and over the carved wooden grip. The dagger's hollow-ground triangular blade, with a wickedly acute point, would be deadly in close combat. Note the brass inserts in the guard and pommel.

The hilt of the rondel dagger is as secure a design as any. The round guard and pommel both protect and provide reassuring containment for the wielder's hand. The textured grip feels secure as well.

Large, disk-shaped pommel

MEDIEVAL KNIFE-FIGHTING TECHNIQUES

An illustration from a 1467 fencing manual by Hans Talhoffer, a fighting master of the French school. It shows a variety of dagger strikes and defenses. As the images show, the techniques are designed chiefly for the rondel dagger, with its disk-shaped guard and pommel and triangular thrusting blade. Manuals such as this are our best sources for the combat traditions of the Middle Ages.

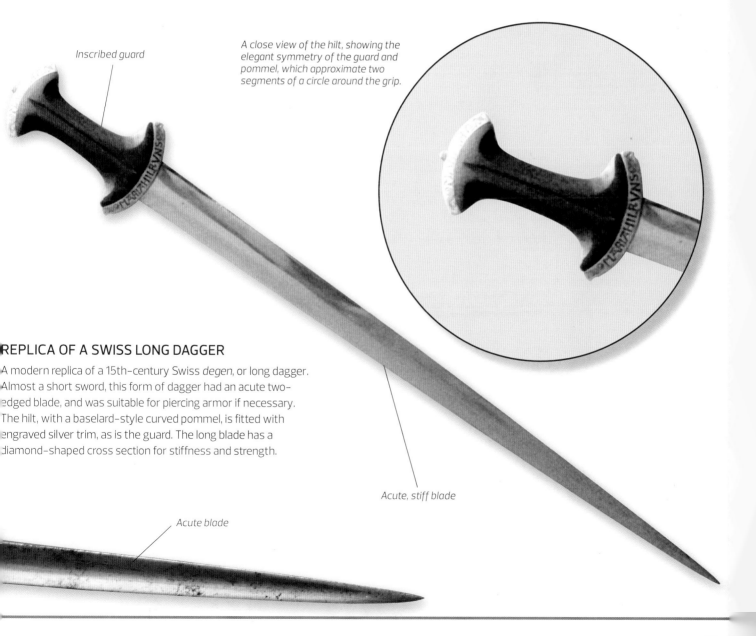

Inscribed guard

A close view of the hilt, showing the elegant symmetry of the guard and pommel, which approximate two segments of a circle around the grip.

REPLICA OF A SWISS LONG DAGGER

A modern replica of a 15th-century Swiss *degen*, or long dagger. Almost a short sword, this form of dagger had an acute two-edged blade, and was suitable for piercing armor if necessary. The hilt, with a baselard-style curved pommel, is fitted with engraved silver trim, as is the guard. The long blade has a diamond-shaped cross section for stiffness and strength.

Acute, stiff blade

Acute blade

Renaissance Daggers

During the Renaissance, the dagger gained new stature as a weapon, for reasons including the advent of firearms and the recognition in Italian city-states that, when swords were banned, daggers could be more than adequate replacements, not least because they could be magnificently decorated and easily wielded in crowded urban settings. In 15th-century Italy, the *cinquedea*—so called because the blade was generally five fingers across at its base—became the street weapon of choice for young aristocrats, while sword-hilt daggers and rondels also gave birth to the stiletto, the pure thrusting dagger. Such inexpensive weapons as the ballock knife continued to see wide use, but increasingly ornate daggers designed to assert their owners' wealth and taste became increasingly prominent. Some were designed by famed painters and sculptors.

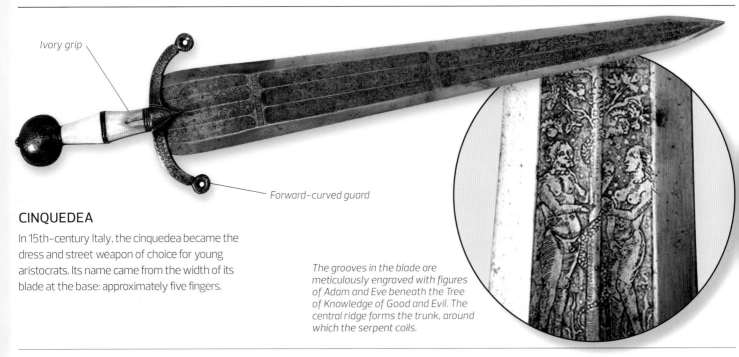

Ivory grip

Forward-curved guard

CINQUEDEA

In 15th-century Italy, the cinquedea became the dress and street weapon of choice for young aristocrats. Its name came from the width of its blade at the base: approximately five fingers.

The grooves in the blade are meticulously engraved with figures of Adam and Eve beneath the Tree of Knowledge of Good and Evil. The central ridge forms the trunk, around which the serpent coils.

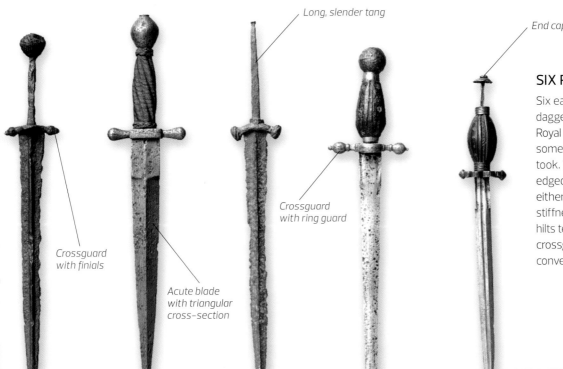

Long, slender tang

End cap for missing pommel

SIX RENAISSANCE DAGGERS

Six early Renaissance sword-hilt daggers from the collections of the Royal Armory of Sweden, illustrating some of the styles this type of knife took. While all the blades are doubled-edged, with acute blade profiles and either center ridges or fullers to add stiffness for penetrating power, the hilts tend to have finials on their crossguards and round pommels and convex handles for sure grip.

Crossguard with ring guard

Crossguard with finials

Acute blade with triangular cross-section

One-piece wooden hilt

Tapered grip

The juncture of a ballock knifes blade and hilt, minus the tang that would have inserted into the grip.

Metal washer on pommel

Anatomically suggestive guard

Heavily corroded blade

Acute blade tip, corroded by seawater

The ballock dagger was often worn across the front of its owner's hips, highlighting the anatomical joke. Victorian scholars renamed the knife the "kidney dagger" to avoid sexual connotations.

KNIVES FROM THE *MARY ROSE*

Until capsizing in battle in the English Channel in 1545, the *Mary Rose* was one of the largest ships in the young English navy, built solely for combat and equipped with the novel design feature of gun ports (which may have played a role in the ship's demise). In 1982, a vast marine archaeology project began to recover the remains of the ship and its artifacts. Among them were many ballock knives—mostly hilts, since the steel blades had largely corroded away. These remains show not only how common such daggers were, but also how the hilts were fitted to the blades.

Acute blade tip

PORTRAIT OF HENRY VIII BY HOLBEIN

A famed portrait of King Henry VIII of England by Hans Holbein, from about 1537–1547. Henry patronized Holbein and his workshop for many years, resulting in some of the finest portraiture of the British monarchy. In this painting, the king stands sturdily, confident in his power. At his belt hangs a long sword-hilt dagger with pommel, guard, and scabbard fittings of gold. Since swords were both unwieldy in crowded or heavily furnished rooms and more threatening than daggers, they were often banned indoors.

ITALIAN DAGGER

A splendid Italian Renaissance dagger from about 1510, with the remains of its sheath. Styled like a rapier, it has forward-curved quillons and a ring guard on only one side of the blade so that the other could rest comfortably against the wearer's body when tucked into a belt. The dagger would be held with the ring guard to the outside, adding protection to the otherwise exposed back of the wielder's hand. At the base of the blade is a short *ricasso*, or unsharpened section, which both serves as a bolster and allows the wielder to wrap a forefinger around the quillons.

The guard of the dagger resembles that of an early rapier, with forward-turned quillons and a ring guard to protect the back of the wielder's hand. Maker's marks are impressed in the ricasso portion of the blade.

Intricately formed pommel

Remains of sheath

DAGGER OF JEAN PARISOT DE VALLETTE

An extraordinary dagger gifted to a remarkable man. In 1565, Philip II of Spain gave this dagger to Jean Parisot de Vallette, Grand Master of the Order of St. John, also known as the Knights Hospitallers and the Knights of Malta. In that year, Vallette led the defenders of Malta in a successful three-month resistance to a siege by Ottoman Turks. For this feat of generalship—his forces were badly outnumbered and outgunned—Vallette became the toast of Europe. Declining an offer to serve as a Cardinal, he founded the city of Valletta, now the capital of Malta, and died peacefully in his sleep in 1568. The dagger is a superb pairing of Baroque design and clean functionality, with ornate chasing on the gold and enamel hilt and an effective double-edged blade with a diamond cross-section and narrow central fuller.

The dagger's ornate hilt, of carved gold, enamel, and gold repoussé, is both opulent in its Baroque styling and functional in that its pommel and guard are balanced and effective.

Intricately formed, enameled gold pommel

Central fuller on the stiff, acute blade

The Main Gauche

In the later Renaissance, the introduction of firearms and the resulting decline in the use of armor led to the advent of the rapier, a sword with a narrow, acute, double-edged blade that was up to four feet long and often fitted with an elaborate guard. Early rapier fighting often involved holding a small buckler in the off hand, but in time a parrying dagger, designed not only to block rapier thrusts but to "catch" an opponent's blade and deliver swift and deadly close-range strikes, became the norm. This form of dagger, called a *main gauche*, or left hand, to indicate its purpose as a secondary weapon, require a stiff blade and a guard capable of protecting the wielder's hand from the blade of a rapier. In due course, a variety of ingenious means to trap opponents' blades were designed into these daggers.

Forward-curved quillons

Textured grip

LEFT-HANDED DAGGER

A left-handed dagger, designed to be used in conjunction with a sword. These daggers, like the 18th-century French one shown, sometimes had substantial down-curved quillons that could be used to trap the opponent's blade long enough to get in a sword thrust.

A view of the blade emerging from the hilt. The raised central ridge stiffens and strengthens the blade for parrying swords, which the forward-curved quillons can then trap.

SPANISH MAIN GAUCHE

Another main gauche, or left-handed dagger, this one from 17th-century Spain. The weapon has a 13½-inch blade with a cutout near the hilt to trap an opponent's blade. The wire-wound grip is short because the user's thumb would be extended to the blade itself, though the hand would be fairly protected by the large guard.

Intricate décor on scabbard

Long, stout quillons

GERMAN MAIN GAUCHE

A classic Northern European main gauche, made in Germany in the 16th century. Its long quillons could be used to parry and catch an opponent's rapier, and its ring guard provides added protection to the back of the wielder's hand. The pommel is balanced to both eye and hand, and the blade, with a central fuller and wickedly acute point, would be effective for counterstrikes as well as parrying.

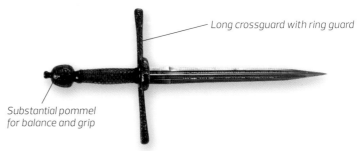

Long crossguard with ring guard

Substantial pommel for balance and grip

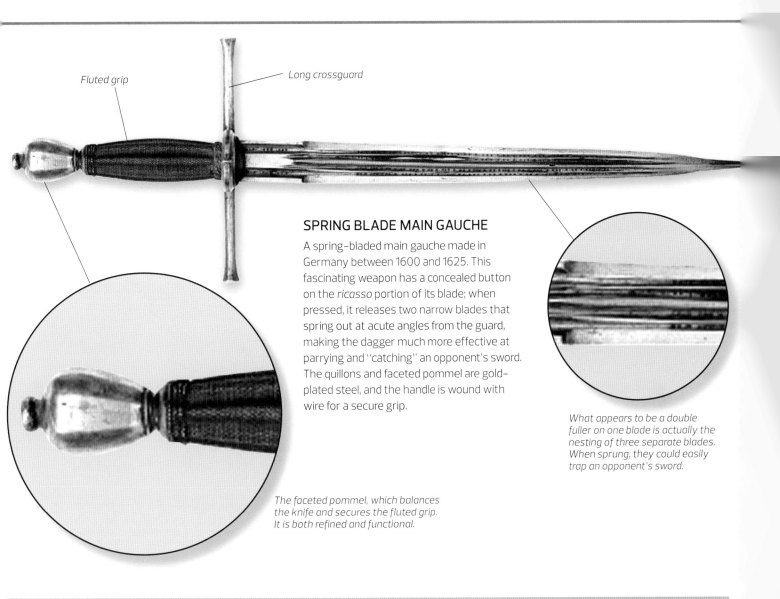

Fluted grip

Long crossguard

SPRING BLADE MAIN GAUCHE

A spring-bladed main gauche made in Germany between 1600 and 1625. This fascinating weapon has a concealed button on the *ricasso* portion of its blade; when pressed, it releases two narrow blades that spring out at acute angles from the guard, making the dagger much more effective at parrying and "catching" an opponent's sword. The quillons and faceted pommel are gold-plated steel, and the handle is wound with wire for a secure grip.

What appears to be a double fuller on one blade is actually the nesting of three separate blades. When sprung, they could easily trap an opponent's sword.

The faceted pommel, which balances the knife and secures the fluted grip. It is both refined and functional.

THE ART OF RAPIER AND DAGGER

An illustration from a Dutch fencing manual from 1595, showing two duelists fighting with rapier and dagger. The daggers appear to be of the classic Swiss variety, while the rapiers are sturdy combat weapons with broad blades and substantial guards. The art of fighting with rapier and dagger was studied intently during the Renaissance, but fell out of favor with the rise of the civilian small sword, which was lethally stiff and acute, and also so nimble in the hand that it made the dagger redundant.

The Gabor Dagger

King Gustavus Adolphus of Sweden (who ruled from 1611 until his death in battle in 1632), was one of the most dynamic and farsighted of European warrior-kings. He was a superb general who made the Swedish army into a model force during the Thirty Years' War. His aggressive tactics, based on rapid movement, mobile artillery, and well-integrated and systematically equipped infantry and cavalry, made Sweden a major European power. He is the only Swedish ruler granted the epithet "the Great." His prominence earned him many gifts, but perhaps none was more spectacular than a set of weapons sent him by Bethlen Gábor, a fellow Protestant and a Prince of Transylvania. The matching set of mace, sabre, and dagger, all of Ottoman design, are a remarkable blending of the martial and the decorative. The dagger and sabre have blades of the most sought-after blade material in history: Damascus steel.

Hilt inlaid with turquoise and rubies

THE GÁBOR DAGGER UNSHEATHED
The relatively unadorned blade contrasts sharply with the magnificently decorated hilt —but the blade has its own visual interest. Forged from damascus steel, also known as "watered steel," it is covered with organic patterns that result from the distinctive organic materials included in the alloy. Those who claim to make "watered steel" now are merely doing pattern welding—the secret of making true damascus steel was lost in the 18th century.

Decorative guard extends over the top of the sheath

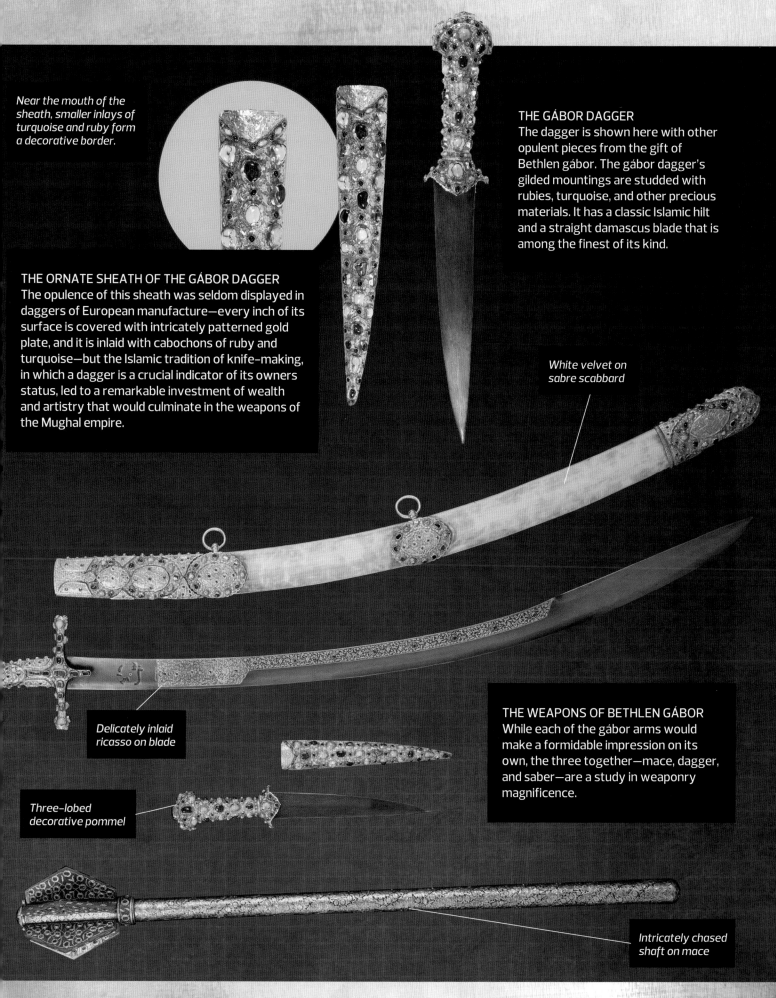

Near the mouth of the sheath, smaller inlays of turquoise and ruby form a decorative border.

THE GÁBOR DAGGER

The dagger is shown here with other opulent pieces from the gift of Bethlen gábor. The gábor dagger's gilded mountings are studded with rubies, turquoise, and other precious materials. It has a classic Islamic hilt and a straight damascus blade that is among the finest of its kind.

THE ORNATE SHEATH OF THE GÁBOR DAGGER

The opulence of this sheath was seldom displayed in daggers of European manufacture—every inch of its surface is covered with intricately patterned gold plate, and it is inlaid with cabochons of ruby and turquoise—but the Islamic tradition of knife-making, in which a dagger is a crucial indicator of its owners status, led to a remarkable investment of wealth and artistry that would culminate in the weapons of the Mughal empire.

White velvet on sabre scabbard

Delicately inlaid ricasso on blade

THE WEAPONS OF BETHLEN GÁBOR

While each of the gábor arms would make a formidable impression on its own, the three together—mace, dagger, and saber—are a study in weaponry magnificence.

Three-lobed decorative pommel

Intricately chased shaft on mace

Later Renaissance Daggers

As the Renaissance unfolded, edged weapons increasingly became civilian mainstays, worn about by gentlemen—or those pretending to the status of gentleman—and richly adorned to indicate their owners' wealth and taste. Sumptuary laws limited the wearing of certain clothes and weapons—especially swords—to the upper classes, so daggers became even more prominent as weapons of self-defense and fashion accessories. Portraits of Renaissance princes and courtiers often feature such ornate daggers tucked into or suspended from belts. Edged blades remained popular, but the stiletto knife, designed purely as a stabbing spike, was widely used as well, and exotically designed weapons that combined blades with firearms became collector's pieces.

LANDSKNECHT DAGGER

A German dagger from the early 16th century, of the kind that might have been used by Swiss and German mercenaries called *landsknechts*, or "servants of the land." The prominent pommel narrows to a grip wrapped in wire. The blackened iron sheath, ornamented with a maskaron, also contains a small utility knife and a skewer for eating or using as an awl. This dagger is at once a combat knife and a campaign tool.

The maskaron, or stylized human face, on the scabbard. Such decorations were common in the Renaissance, having been copied or adapted from originals found in Roman architectural remains.

Reinforced scabbard

Blackened iron sheath

Oversized pommel

Forward-angled quillons

SWISS DAGGER WITH EXQUISITE SCABBARD

An early 16th-century Swiss dagger with a magnificent sheath. While the knife itself displays the classic hilt pattern of a Swiss dagger, with curved pommel and guard, the sheath reveals how a Renaissance dagger could be used as a statement of status and taste. Because the dagger would be worn horizontally in its owner's belt, the intricate gold-plated openwork on the sheath "reads" along the axis of the blade.

A close view of the intricate openwork on the scabbard. Such craftsmanship did not come cheap, making a dagger such as this a piece of conspicuous consumption.

Integrated grip and guard

Ergonomically turned grip

Ornate finial on scabbard tip

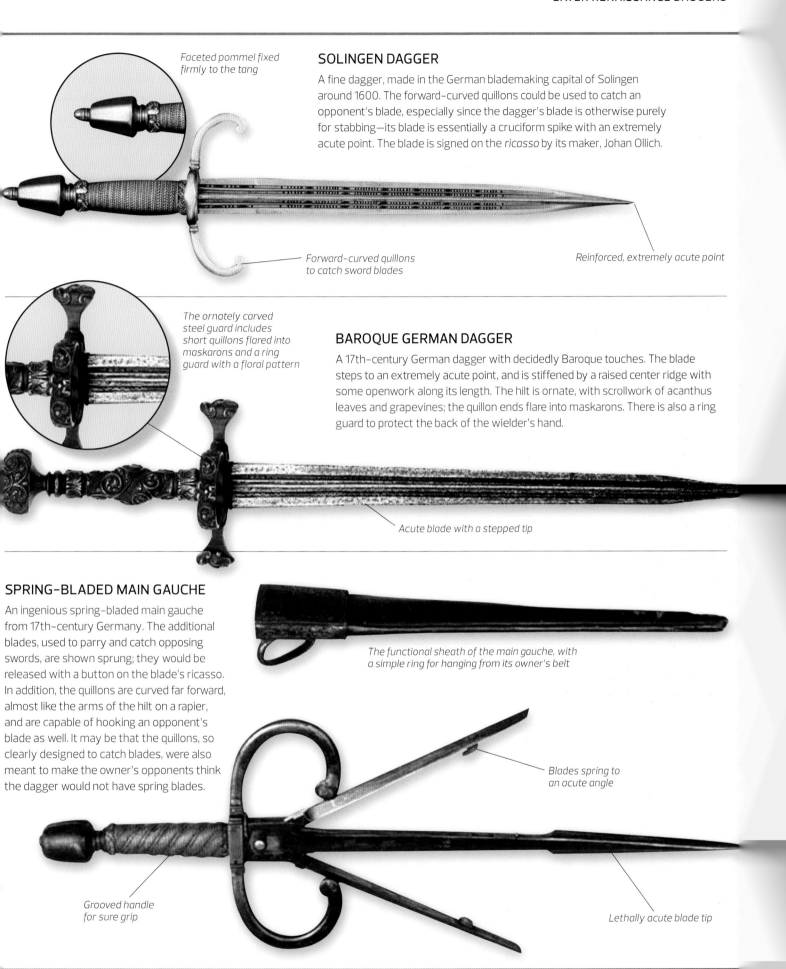

Faceted pommel fixed firmly to the tang

SOLINGEN DAGGER

A fine dagger, made in the German blademaking capital of Solingen around 1600. The forward-curved quillons could be used to catch an opponent's blade, especially since the dagger's blade is otherwise purely for stabbing—its blade is essentially a cruciform spike with an extremely acute point. The blade is signed on the *ricasso* by its maker, Johan Ollich.

Forward-curved quillons to catch sword blades

Reinforced, extremely acute point

The ornately carved steel guard includes short quillons flared into maskarons and a ring guard with a floral pattern

BAROQUE GERMAN DAGGER

A 17th-century German dagger with decidedly Baroque touches. The blade steps to an extremely acute point, and is stiffened by a raised center ridge with some openwork along its length. The hilt is ornate, with scrollwork of acanthus leaves and grapevines; the quillon ends flare into maskarons. There is also a ring guard to protect the back of the wielder's hand.

Acute blade with a stepped tip

SPRING-BLADED MAIN GAUCHE

An ingenious spring-bladed main gauche from 17th-century Germany. The additional blades, used to parry and catch opposing swords, are shown sprung; they would be released with a button on the blade's ricasso. In addition, the quillons are curved far forward, almost like the arms of the hilt on a rapier, and are capable of hooking an opponent's blade as well. It may be that the quillons, so clearly designed to catch blades, were also meant to make the owner's opponents think the dagger would not have spring blades.

The functional sheath of the main gauche, with a simple ring for hanging from its owner's belt

Blades spring to an acute angle

Grooved handle for sure grip

Lethally acute blade tip

Wire-wrapped grip

Fluted pommel

Fullers stiffen the acute blade

CLASSIC GERMAN DAGGER

Perhaps the most classic dagger form of all: an austere sword-hilt dagger from early 17th-century Germany. The acute blade has a raised center ridge, with fine decorative openwork alongside. The restrained hilt is a beautifully balanced cruciform pattern, with slightly flared quillons, a small ring guard, and a fluted pommel. The grip is wrapped with steel wire.

TWO GERMAN DISK DAGGERS

Two 15th-century daggers from the Swedish Royal Armory. One is a classic rondel, with disk-shaped guard and pommel and a stiletto-type blade; the other is a curious hybrid, with the guard of a ballock knife and the pommel of a rondel. Two small forward-angled guards supplement the ballock guard. Both weapons are made purely for stabbing, not for parrying.

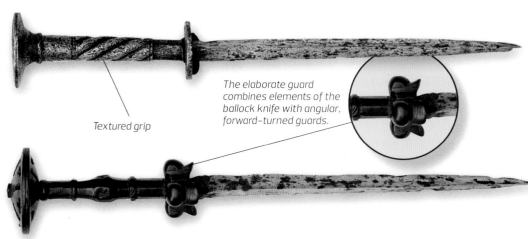

Textured grip

The elaborate guard combines elements of the ballock knife with angular, forward-turned guards.

ITALIAN DAGGER

An ornate 17th-century dagger, likely of Italian manufacture. It has a stately hilt of silver paneled with tortoise shell, and a small joint section between the understated crossguard and the acute, partially fullered blade. This sort of finely made blade was more fashion accessory than weapon; the ornate hilt, as the most visible part of the dagger when worn, received the most artistic attention.

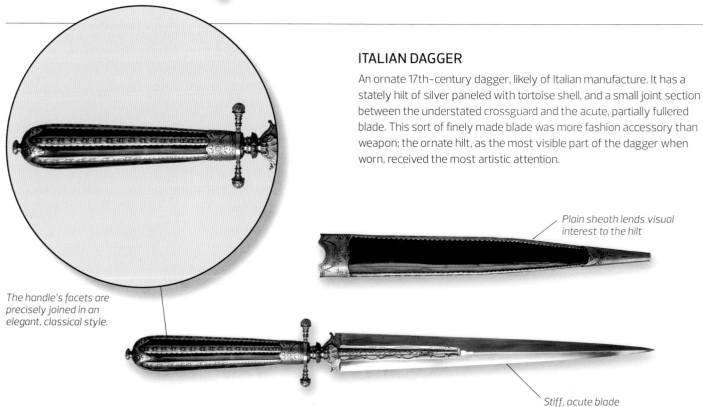

The handle's facets are precisely joined in an elegant, classical style.

Plain sheath lends visual interest to the hilt

Stiff, acute blade

Scalloped shell guard

Fluted, gold-plated pommel for balance

Forward-curved quillons

This combination dagger features a brass firing pin, which is laid flush with the edges of the blade.

The exquisitely carved openwork overlay of the firing mechanism which looks delicate but is actually robustly made.

Velvet trim on sheath

WHEEL-LOCK DAGGERS

In the late Renaissance, combination weapons became fashionable among those who could afford them. These two combination daggers and wheel-lock pistols would have been prized possessions and conversation pieces as well as means of self-defense. One has a large shell guard; both have forward-curved quillons, gold filigree work on the *ricasso*, and fluted pommels.

Medieval and Renaissance Pole Arms and Halberds

In the early Middle Ages, one of the most effective battlefield weapons was the battle-axe. Unlike the mostly straight, two-edged swords of the era, which might be expertly balanced and capable of thrusting attacks, an axe focused tremendous shearing force at the point of impact, and a well-made axe blade could cut through chain mail and leather armor. Vikings were perhaps most famous for their use of axes, though they venerated swords more and made some of the finest blades of the era. During the Crusades, European knights encountered Islamic axes, which were often as beautiful as they were effective in battle. With the advent of plate armor in the thirteenth century, however, the axe lost some of its luster in Europe, as did the traditional arming sword. In the Islamic world and the Mughal Empire of India, however, axes remained mainstays of the arsenal.

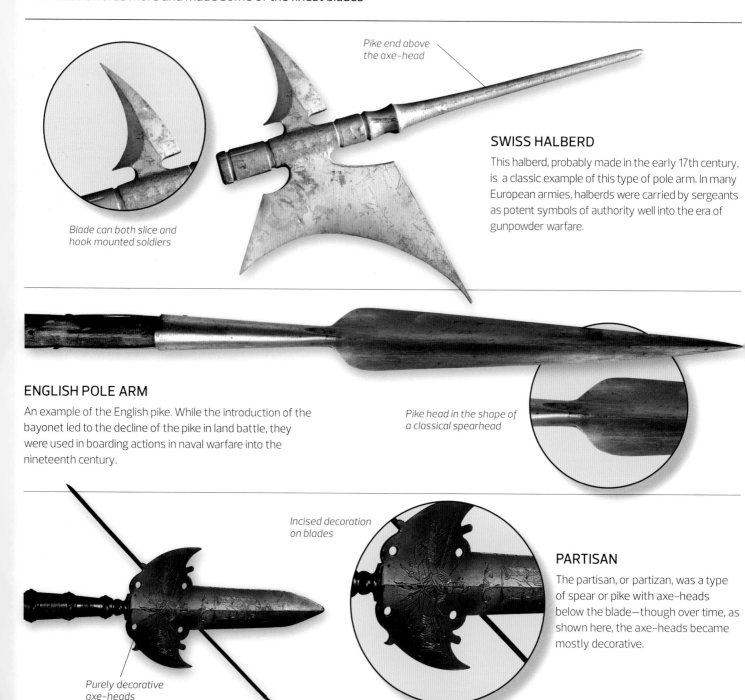

Pike end above the axe-head

Blade can both slice and hook mounted soldiers

SWISS HALBERD

This halberd, probably made in the early 17th century, is a classic example of this type of pole arm. In many European armies, halberds were carried by sergeants as potent symbols of authority well into the era of gunpowder warfare.

ENGLISH POLE ARM

An example of the English pike. While the introduction of the bayonet led to the decline of the pike in land battle, they were used in boarding actions in naval warfare into the nineteenth century.

Pike head in the shape of a classical spearhead

Incised decoration on blades

PARTISAN

The partisan, or partizan, was a type of spear or pike with axe-heads below the blade—though over time, as shown here, the axe-heads became mostly decorative.

Purely decorative axe-heads

ITALIAN POLE ARM

The glaive, or fouchard, is a European pole arm with a single-edged knife-like blade, usually 18 inches, fixed to a shaft of up to 7 feet in length. Some versions—like the Italian example shown here—also had one or more hooks to snag riders from the saddle. As with the halberd, glaives took on a more ceremonial role as firearms changed European warfare.

Intricate etching on blade

Socket mount to fix blade on shaft

Long pike blade atop axe-head

Acute slicing hook opposite axe-head

ENGLISH HALBERD

A fine example of the halberd dating from the 16th century and probably of English origin, this weapon has a typically long, tapering blade, and a clearly defined axe-head.

Straight axe edge

The substantial head is affixed to the shaft with three large rivets through the tang.

FRENCH POLE ARM

An 18th-century French pole arm with a blade in the shape of a fleur-de-lis, symbol of the French monarchy.

Sturdy socket mount

Detailed etching on the blade depicts royal regalia as well as decorative patterns

Steel reinforcement plate on upper portion of shaft

SWISS POLE ARM

The head of a Swiss pole arm. The effectiveness of Swiss infantry equipped with pole arms, particularly the pike, made them among the most feared warriors in Europe during the fourteenth and fifteenth centuries.

Medieval and Renaissance Maces and Flails

The advent of plate armor in the 13th century resulted in a somewhat ironic development in hand weapons: the return of the club, in the form of the mace. While bladed weapons had to evolve significantly to deal with the relative impenetrability of plate armor, maces proved devastatingly effective against it. The blow of a well-aimed mace can do tremendous damage through plate armor, because the force of the strike is simply transferred through the armor to the body underneath. Later maces often featured flanges—raised, narrow striking surfaces that further concentrated the force of impact, to the point that such maces could rupture plate armor completely. As the Middle Ages gave way to the Renaissance, the mace became less a weapon than a symbol, often denoting rank or responsibility. To this day, ceremonial maces figure in the rituals of such institutions as universities, civic organizations, and even the British Parliament.

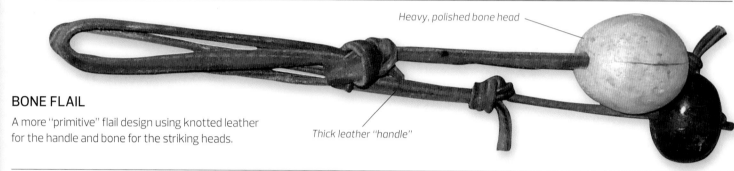

Heavy, polished bone head

BONE FLAIL

A more "primitive" flail design using knotted leather for the handle and bone for the striking heads.

Thick leather "handle"

LEATHER FLAIL

An unusual flail with a knotted hardwood striking head attached to a wooden handle by leather straps. A leather thong secured the weapon to its owners wrist.

"Chain" of bundled leather strips

Leather mounting on shaft

Carved hardwood head would be ineffective against armor

Spiked head

MORGENSTERN

One of the most common types of sixteenth-century European maces was the morgenstern, which had a spiked head attached to the shaft. The morgenstern was used extensively by the Habsburgs, and the name comes from either the German for "morning star," likely a reference to its sunlike spiked head, or as a grim joke based on the fact that the weapon was often used in dawn raids on enemy encampments.

Flanged and spiked head are purely aesthetic and symbolic.

Intricately etched silver-plated shaft

CEREMONIAL MACE

The mace as a real weapon went out of use with the disappearance of heavy armor. Ceremonial maces are often made from precious metals such as silver, sometimes with elaborate engravings.

ENGLISH FLAIL

An English flail from the time of King Henry VII (r. 1485–1509). While similar to the morgenstern in design, flails usually had several lengths of chain or spiked balls attached to a shaft, although this example has only one. A major advantage of the flail was that it could be swung over or around a knight's shield.

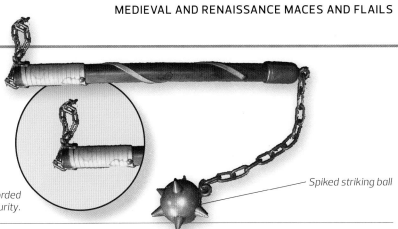

Spiked striking ball

Wooden shaft has a simple corded grip with a wrist strap for security.

RUSSIAN FLAILS

Metal military flails used by 18th-century Russian peasant insurgents. The social and economic status of the maker is reflected in the crude design of these weapons.

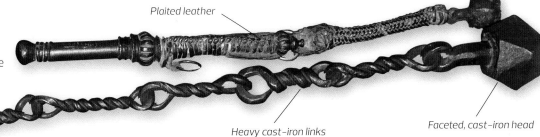

Plaited leather

Heavy cast-iron links

Faceted, cast-iron head

MORNING STAR MACE

This English mace from the 1400s gets its name from the shape of its spiked head. This unusual example has a metal spring neck and a wooden handle making it something of a hybrid between a mace and a flail.

The flail's cast-iron head has five short, durable spikes for penetrating power. The spring shaft would add velocity, and hence force, to each strike.

Wrist strap

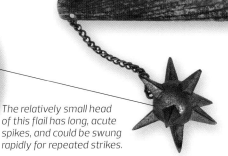

The relatively small head of this flail has long, acute spikes, and could be swung rapidly for repeated strikes.

Simple wooden handle

ENGLISH FLAIL

This variation on the English flail has a wooden handle and a slender chain making it lighter to wield.

Silver grip mounted to wooden shaft

RARE BULWA

A rare Caucasian Commander's Bulwa (Russian Mace) with an oval soapstone head capped with silver and a silver-mounted wooden shaft.

The Islamic Dagger

A Legacy of Daggers

The great empires and peoples of the Islamic world had traditions of knife-making and close combat that predated Islam, but the aesthetic and codes of conduct that accompanied Islamic civilization led to a remarkable legacy of daggers as both effective weapons and magnificent art objects.

From the ornate mountings of Turkish *yataghans* and Arabian *jambiyas* to the exquisite daggers of the Persian Safavid and Indo-Persian Mughal civilizations, the variety and beauty of Islamic daggers are unmatched. Many of the finest examples not only display remarkable decorative work but also have blades of Damascus steel, considered by many to be the finest blade steel ever manufactured.

A WALL OF OMANI KHANJARS
The *khanjar* is the emblematic knife of Oman. The double-edged blade of a khanjar is housed in a silver sheath, which is hung from a belt decorated with silver. Though a national symbol of Oman, the khanjar is found throughout much of the Islamic world.

Persian and Turkish Daggers

In many Islamic traditions, the dagger is an object of tremendous symbolic and material value, and extraordinary artistry is lavished on knives. This is certainly true of the daggers of Persia, especially the Safavid Dynasty of the 16th to 18th centuries, and those of the Ottoman Empire. Many of these knives have superb, organically patterned blades of true Damascus, or "watered" steel, the most prized blade metal in history. They also were adorned with exquisite decorative patterns, inlays of gold and gemstones, and intricate designs that often employed graceful calligraphy.

Inlay of semiprecious stones

Etched-metal sheath

PERSIAN KHANJAR

This 17th-century dagger has all the hallmarks of quality. The handle is inlaid with semiprecious stones of many colors while the sheath and blade have deeply etched linear and floral decorations.

Linear-pattern etching on blade

Unsheathed dagger

PERSIAN THREE-BLADED DAGGER

In this 18th-century example of a Persian three-bladed dagger, the blade is made up of three leaves that spring apart when the weapon is pulled from its sheath. The blades are decorated with silver and gold damascening.

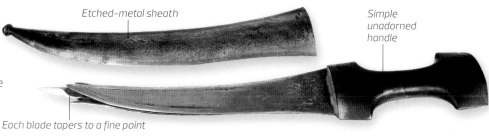

Etched-metal sheath

Simple unadorned handle

Each blade tapers to a fine point

TURKISH SÜRMENE FIGHTING KNIFE

A traditional Sürmene fighting knife from Turkey, where it was used in the north along the coast of the Black Sea. The lethally acute blade has an incised silver bolster; the hilt is riveted with horn scales. A small utility/sharpening knife also fits into the sheath. Though elegant, this is very much a fighting knife.

Utility knife

Incised-metal bolster

TOPKAPI DAGGER

A fine dagger made in the workshop of the Topkapi Palace, home of the Ottoman Sultan, in the early 17th century. The elaborate hilt is of ornately carved ivory set with two rubies and a cabochon of turquoise. The acute blade has four grooves and is housed in a unadorned silver sheath. This is a weapon of understated elegance.

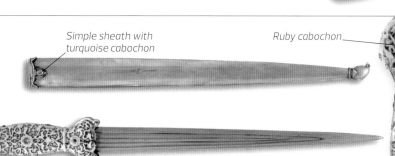

Simple sheath with turquoise cabochon

Ruby cabochon

Carved-ivory handle

Turquoise cabochon

Daggers of the Ottoman Empire

At its peak in the 16th century, the Ottoman Empire encompassed lands from stretching from Central Europe to the Persian Gulf and down into most of the Mediterranean coastal regions. This vast panoply of territories included many different weapons traditions and a wide variety of daggers. One of the most famed is the *kindjal*, the traditional dagger of the Caucasus region. This double-edged straight knife is as elegant as it is deadly.

Also prominent in the Ottoman armory was the *yataghan* dagger, a distinctive single-edged knife with a pommel featuring two "ears," like the joint of a bone. Both designs were adopted through large swaths of the empire.

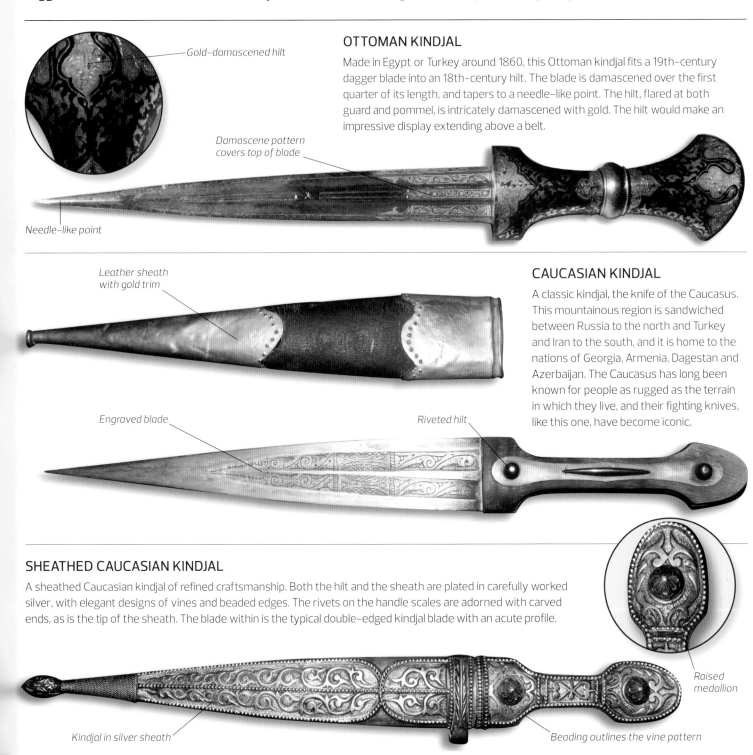

OTTOMAN KINDJAL

Made in Egypt or Turkey around 1860, this Ottoman kindjal fits a 19th-century dagger blade into an 18th-century hilt. The blade is damascened over the first quarter of its length, and tapers to a needle-like point. The hilt, flared at both guard and pommel, is intricately damascened with gold. The hilt would make an impressive display extending above a belt.

Gold-damascened hilt

Damascene pattern covers top of blade

Needle-like point

CAUCASIAN KINDJAL

A classic kindjal, the knife of the Caucasus. This mountainous region is sandwiched between Russia to the north and Turkey and Iran to the south, and it is home to the nations of Georgia, Armenia, Dagestan and Azerbaijan. The Caucasus has long been known for people as rugged as the terrain in which they live, and their fighting knives, like this one, have become iconic.

Leather sheath with gold trim

Engraved blade

Riveted hilt

SHEATHED CAUCASIAN KINDJAL

A sheathed Caucasian kindjal of refined craftsmanship. Both the hilt and the sheath are plated in carefully worked silver, with elegant designs of vines and beaded edges. The rivets on the handle scales are adorned with carved ends, as is the tip of the sheath. The blade within is the typical double-edged kindjal blade with an acute profile.

Raised medallion

Kindjal in silver sheath

Beading outlines the vine pattern

ORNATE KINDJAL FROM A SHOOTING SET

Created as part of a hunting set, this magnificent 18th-century Ottoman kindjal was created as part of a hunting set and fits into the butt of a matching rifle. The hilt is of gold-plated silver and studded with rubies and emeralds. The blade, decorated with gold wire in a technique similar to damascene, is divided for most of its length into three parts, with leaf designs inlaid with precious stones where they join near the hilt.

The blade's decorative work is "false damascene," a technique in which gold wire is pressed into ornate designs. Note the artistry in the inlay of both smooth polished and faceted emeralds and rubies, some used as borders and others within design elements.

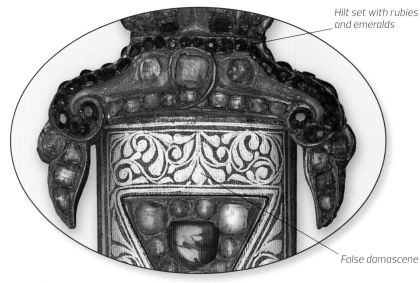

Hilt set with rubies and emeralds

False damascene

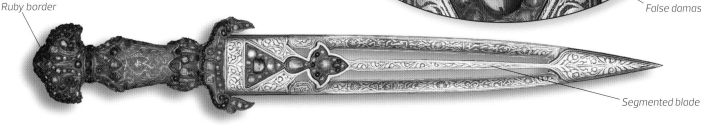

Ruby border

Segmented blade

BOSNIAN YATAGHAN DAGGER

Bosnia has long been a conflicted region, lying along with other Balkan regions in what was for centuries a restless Ottoman frontier on the doorstep of Europe. This Bosnian yataghan dagger made in 1889. The hilt has ivory scales with the classic yataghan "ears," and is inlaid with precious and semiprecious stones. The blade is housed in a sheath wrapped in gold foil.

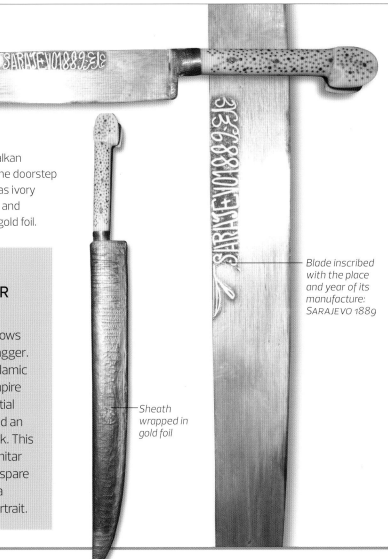

Single-edged blade tapers to a fine point

Blade inscribed with the place and year of its manufacture: SARAJEVO 1889

Sheath wrapped in gold foil

PORTRAIT OF AN OTTOMAN WARRIOR

A 17th-century Turkish manuscript illustration shows a warrior with hand on dagger. As in other parts of the Islamic world, in the Ottoman Empire the dagger was an essential piece of men's apparel and an important indicator of rank. This warrior also carries a scimitar and a quiver of arrows. A spare dagger sheath occupies a prominent place in the portrait.

Daggers of Arabia and Syria

The dagger is an essential part of men's dress in Arabia and much of the Levant, and in many places strict customs govern its use. For the Bedouin and other desert peoples, the dress dagger is distinct from the ordinary knife in that it serves as a means of self-defense and is only to be drawn in the most extreme circumstances. The *khanjar*, the national knife of Oman, is such a dress knife, and *khanjar* is one of a handful of terms that have come to be used throughout the Islamic world for dress daggers.

Utility knives, which take a variety of forms, might include decorative touches more commonly associated with dress daggers. While dress daggers often have elaborately worked and inlaid hilts of precious metal, utility knives are more likely to have handles with horn or hardwood scales.

ARABIAN TRIPLE DAGGER SET

An Arabian sheath containing three daggers dating from the early 19th century. The daggers have ornate brass handles and are carried in a decorated scabbard.

Scabbard decorated with floral motifs

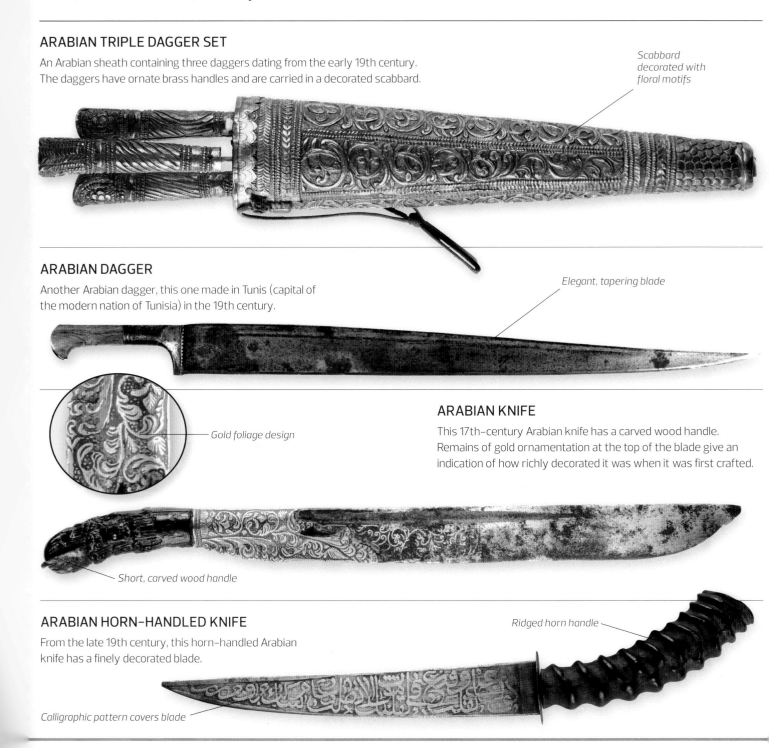

ARABIAN DAGGER

Another Arabian dagger, this one made in Tunis (capital of the modern nation of Tunisia) in the 19th century.

Elegant, tapering blade

Gold foliage design

ARABIAN KNIFE

This 17th-century Arabian knife has a carved wood handle. Remains of gold ornamentation at the top of the blade give an indication of how richly decorated it was when it was first crafted.

Short, carved wood handle

ARABIAN HORN-HANDLED KNIFE

From the late 19th century, this horn-handled Arabian knife has a finely decorated blade.

Ridged horn handle

Calligraphic pattern covers blade

SOLID-SILVER DAGGER

This is an ornate early-20th-century silver dagger made in Arabia. It has a very sharp double-edged blade and its metal sheath is decorated to match the blade.

Engraved silver sheath

Flared grip

Engraved blade matches sheath

SYRIAN DAGGER

A set of three Syrian daggers made in the 19th century. Each has a blade measuring 5¼ inches; two have curved blades and one, a straight blade. The three bone-handled knives fit into a sheath of crocodile skin.

Crocodile-skin sheath

Straight-bladed dagger

Bone handle

SYRIAN KNIFE WITH SHEATH

This Syrian blade from the late 19th century has a carefully shaped sheath, beaded in a style usually associated with the tribes of East Africa.

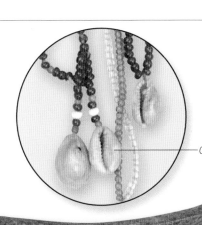

Cowrie-shell trim

Multicolored beading

Bone handle

Curved blade

73

Jambiya

The jambiya is perhaps the most widely known form of Arabian dress dagger; though its blade can take many forms, it is almost always at least slightly curved and single edged, though often with a false edge toward the point. In much of the Arab world, the jambiya is a powerfully symbolic accessory. Not only is it a badge of manhood and cultural identity, it also serves to indicate at a glance the wealth and status of its owner. Since, by custom, jambiyas are not drawn except in life-or-death circumstances, artistic attention is focused on the scabbard and especially the handle, which is often made of precious materials and inlaid with colorful gemstones.

TRADITIONAL JAMBIYA

Worn on the belt, the jambiya is mainly a decorative item, but it is also an efficient fighting knife. The leather sheath of this 18th-century knife has clearly been worn from much use. The blade has a wide fuller and an ornamental gold-colored handle.

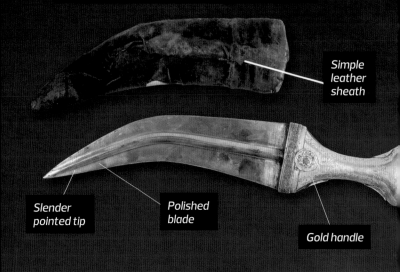

Simple leather sheath

Slender pointed tip

Polished blade

Gold handle

Chalcedony grip

OTTOMAN JAMBIYA

A superb Ottoman jambiya, elegantly fashioned of exquisite materials. The Damascus blade is fitted to a hilt of milky chalcedony, which is trimmed with gold filigree and inlaid with small emeralds and rubies with gold mountings. The sheath is adorned with decorative enamel work and inlaid with scores of precious stones. This dagger is at once regal and restrained.

INDIAN JAMBIYA

This rare Indian jambiya from around 1840 is all steel. The blade is forged in three pieces that spring open when the knife is drawn from its sheath. The central portion is a spike and the outer ones are the conventional curved double-edged blade.

Indian figures

Ball tip to protect blades

Narrow, tubular handle

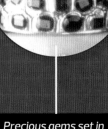

Engraved blades

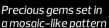

Precious gems set in a mosaic-like pattern

SIMPLE JAMBIYA

This jambiya is a traditional design with a 10-inch curved blade and tooled leather cover over a wooden sheath. The handle is black horn.

Tooled leatherwork

Horn handle

10-inch blade

Curved sheath to match dagger

Sheath in good condition

DAGGERS ON DISPLAY

In many Islamic cultures, jambiyas and other ornamental knives are worn on the belt as a symbol of freedom. These men display their daggers at a festival in Sa'dah, Yemen.

Tubular metal handle

CEREMONIAL JAMBIYA

Judging by its perfect condition and restrained and elegant ornamentation, this jambiya would have been made and worn as a ceremonial piece rather than used for fighting.

Narrow handle with rounded top

Fuller along center of blade

Leather sheath

MODERN JAMBIYA

This Arabian jambiya dates from the 20th century and is shown with its carved leather sheath. It has a bone handle inset with gold-colored medallions.

Daggers of North Africa

When Islam spread rapidly from Arabia across North Africa, with it went the knife styles of the Arabian peninsula. Ever since, the daggers of North Africa have combined native elements with the classic forms of Arabian and Egyptian knives. The most famous of these knives is the *khoumija*, the North African version of the jambiya. As in more eastern regions, this dagger is prominent in traditional men's costume, and its handle and scabbard are often showpieces of the metalworker's or jeweler's art. In the Sahara, nomadic tribesmen generally carry knives that incorporate both utilitarian and combat elements, and the dagger is associated with the virtues of honor, reliability, and resourcefulness.

TUNISIAN DAGGER

A 19th-century Tunisian dagger with a wavy "flaming" blade. Given its Mediterranean coastline and proximity to Italy, Tunisia has long been a crossroads of North African and European cultures. This dagger, with its cruciform hilt and wavy blade, exemplifies that cross-cultural influence. The convex handle ends in a brass pommel, which is matched by the slightly flared quillons.

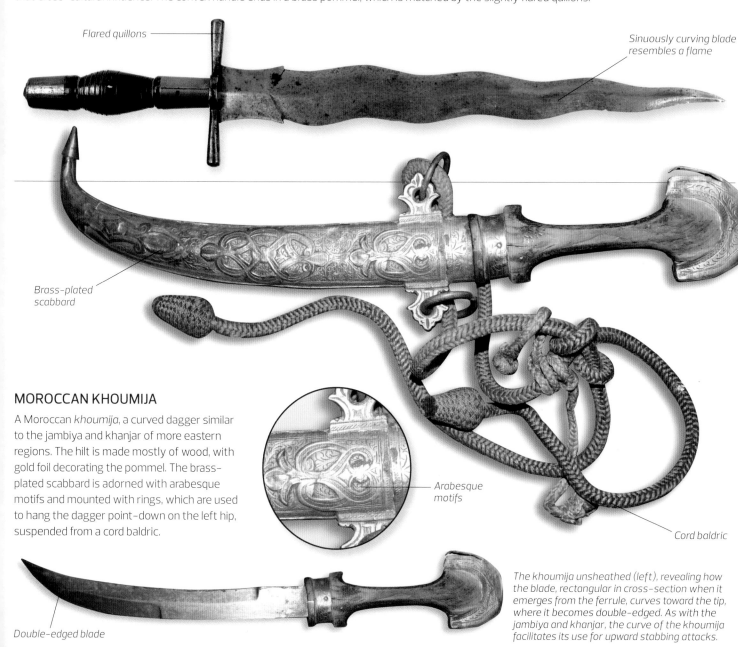

Flared quillons

Sinuously curving blade resembles a flame

Brass-plated scabbard

Arabesque motifs

Cord baldric

MOROCCAN KHOUMIJA

A Moroccan *khoumija*, a curved dagger similar to the jambiya and khanjar of more eastern regions. The hilt is made mostly of wood, with gold foil decorating the pommel. The brass-plated scabbard is adorned with arabesque motifs and mounted with rings, which are used to hang the dagger point-down on the left hip, suspended from a cord baldric.

Double-edged blade

The khoumija unsheathed (left), revealing how the blade, rectangular in cross-section when it emerges from the ferrule, curves toward the tip, where it becomes double-edged. As with the jambiya and khanjar, the curve of the khoumija facilitates its use for upward stabbing attacks.

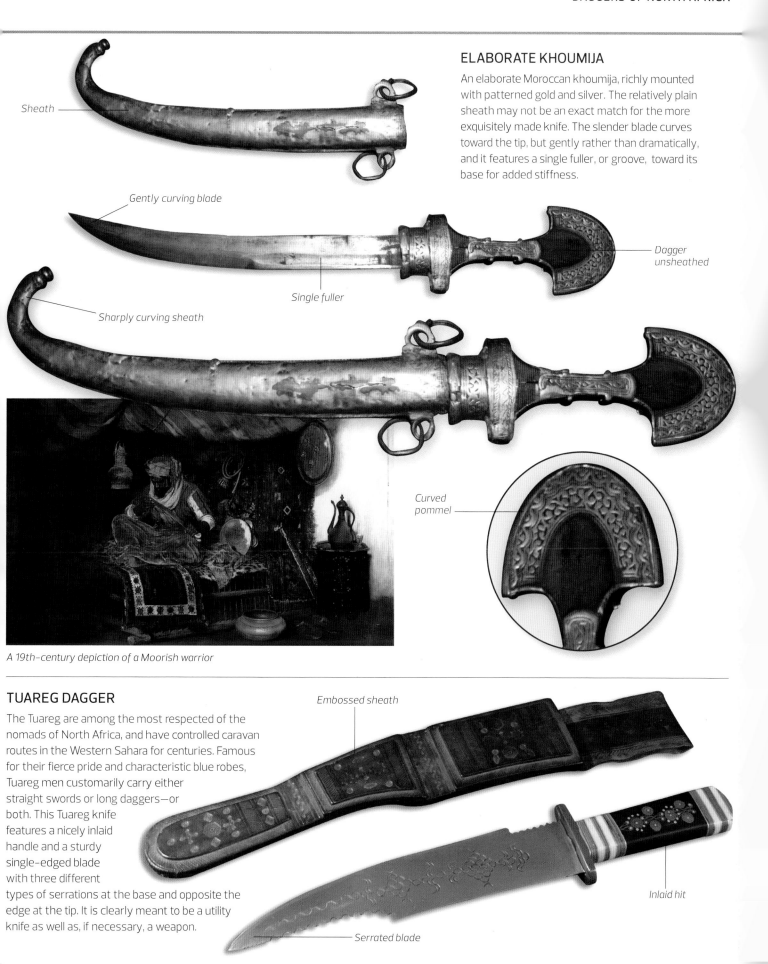

Sheath

ELABORATE KHOUMIJA

An elaborate Moroccan khoumija, richly mounted with patterned gold and silver. The relatively plain sheath may not be an exact match for the more exquisitely made knife. The slender blade curves toward the tip, but gently rather than dramatically, and it features a single fuller, or groove, toward its base for added stiffness.

Gently curving blade

Dagger unsheathed

Single fuller

Sharply curving sheath

Curved pommel

A 19th-century depiction of a Moorish warrior

TUAREG DAGGER

The Tuareg are among the most respected of the nomads of North Africa, and have controlled caravan routes in the Western Sahara for centuries. Famous for their fierce pride and characteristic blue robes, Tuareg men customarily carry either straight swords or long daggers—or both. This Tuareg knife features a nicely inlaid handle and a sturdy single-edged blade with three different types of serrations at the base and opposite the edge at the tip. It is clearly meant to be a utility knife as well as, if necessary, a weapon.

Embossed sheath

Inlaid hit

Serrated blade

Mughal Daggers

There is arguably no more magnificent knife-making legacy than that of the Mughal Empire, which extended over much of the Indian subcontinent from the 16th through the 19th centuries.

Most Mughal rulers, most famously Akbar (1542–1605) tended toward religious tolerance and cultivation of the arts. The resulting confluence of Persian, Indo-Islamic, and Hindu currents led to one of the most remarkable cultural flowerings in world history. Mughal painting and architecture—the Taj Mahal is only one example—have long been considered great artistic traditions, but Mughal arms and armor are often breathtakingly beautiful. Mughal daggers, worn both for self-defense and as works of art, combine fine steel blades with some of the most intricate and luxurious mountings ever made.

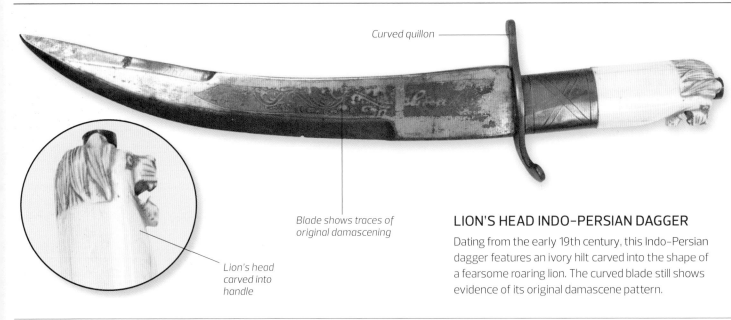

Curved quillon

Blade shows traces of original damascening

Lion's head carved into handle

LION'S HEAD INDO-PERSIAN DAGGER

Dating from the early 19th century, this Indo-Persian dagger features an ivory hilt carved into the shape of a fearsome roaring lion. The curved blade still shows evidence of its original damascene pattern.

CLASSIC MUGHAL DAGGER

Made in the 17th century, this is a classically elegant Mughal dagger. The curved blade, single-edged for most of its length, ends in a double-edged tip with a wickedly acute point, and features a pronounced center ridge with delicate damascene work at the base. The hilt is of jade, inlaid with enamel and semiprecious stones including turquoise and amethyst. At the base of the guard, which is carved in a floral pattern, is a narrow band of coral.

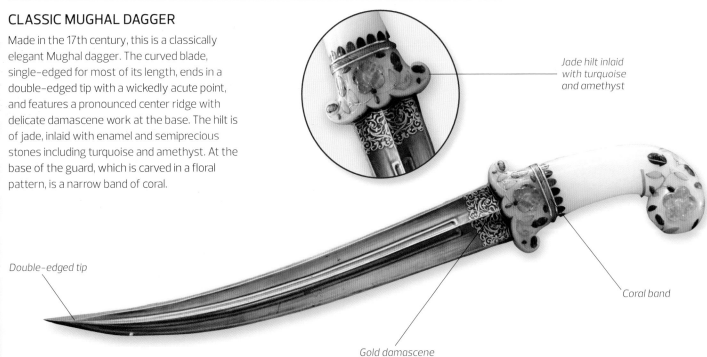

Jade hilt inlaid with turquoise and amethyst

Double-edged tip

Coral band

Gold damascene

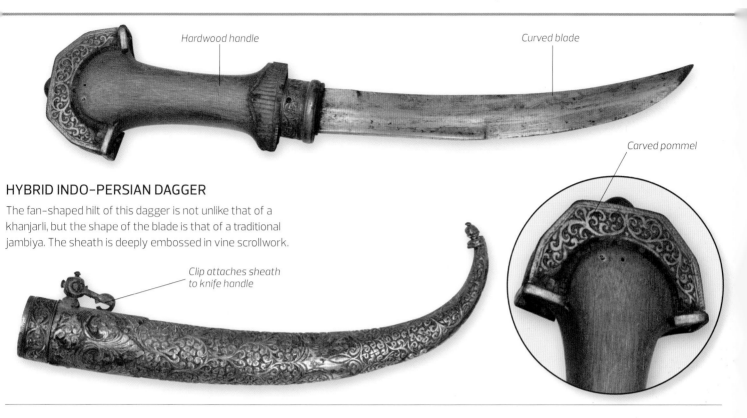

Hardwood handle

Curved blade

Carved pommel

HYBRID INDO-PERSIAN DAGGER

The fan-shaped hilt of this dagger is not unlike that of a khanjarli, but the shape of the blade is that of a traditional jambiya. The sheath is deeply embossed in vine scrollwork.

Clip attaches sheath to knife handle

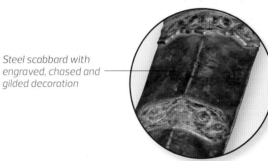

DAMASCUS DAGGER

A distinctive 17th- or 18th-century Mughal dagger with a Damascus steel blade and a jade hilt. The chiseled, angular form of the hilt is somewhat unusual for a Mughal weapon; most have more sinuous and delicate lines. The arabesque inlay on the blade and on the steel sheath, however, is classic Indo-Persian decoration. The straight Damascus blade has a raised center ridge and tapers to a moderately acute point.

Steel scabbard with engraved, chased and gilded decoration

Jade hilt

Gold damascene

INDO-PERSIAN KNIFE

Dating from the late 18th-century, this long-bladed knife has a distinctive curved handle.

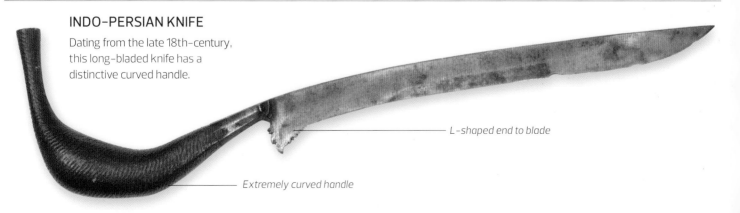

L-shaped end to blade

Extremely curved handle

The Art of the Mughal Knife Handle

Nowhere is the sublime artistry of Mughal daggers more evident than in their handles. Often fashioned of such rare and striking materials as jade, agate and even crystal and adorned with meticulous inlays of gold, silver and precious stones, they nonetheless avoid the ostentation that sometimes crept into the artistic blade mountings of other great traditions. Their characteristic pistol grips were often expertly carved into zoomorphic forms such as horses' and rams' heads. These remarkable mountings stand on their own as remarkable art objects.

RAM'S HEAD HILT

The Mughals can be said to have perfected the art of the zoomorphic pommel. This example, carved in mottled jade in the 17th century, ends in a remarkably detailed and stylized ram's head. The ears and horns emerge in relief, and the latter are expertly striated—even the ram's teeth are rendered individually in a strikingly realistic fashion. The handle is designed to be set into a separate guard, probably with a ferrule of gold–plated or damascened steel.

Mottled jade

Meticulously carved details

REFINED JADE HILT

This elegant hilt, made in about 1800, is of carved and polished jade with a single decorative motif of flowers and vines extending the full length of the piece. The curve of the pistol grip emphasizes the organic quality of the decorative design. The inlay consists of gold and silver, set with rubies, emeralds, sapphires, pearls, coral and glass. An extraordinary display of artistry.

Precious stones form a floral patterned, which is highlighted with gold

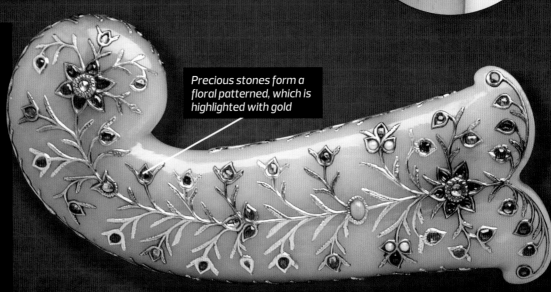

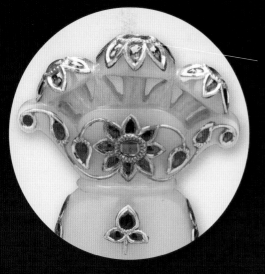

Rubies, emeralds and diamonds form floral pattern

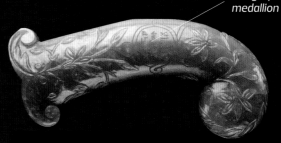

Calligraphic medallion

SIMPLE JADE HILT

A simple, relatively unadorned 18th-century Mughal knife handle. Made of carved and polished jade, it is incised all over with a design of trailing vines; at the midpoint of the grip is a simple medallion with a calligraphic inscription. This hilt distills the classic pistol-grip hilt of the Mughal dagger to its essence.

EXQUISITE WHITE JADE HILT

A regal Mughal hilt from the early 18th century, made entirely of carved and polished white jade—the most sought-after variety of the stone. Rather than turned into a pistol grip, the pommel is capped with an openwork design that echoes the floral motifs of the inlaid decorations, which include gold foil, rubies, emeralds and diamonds. The grip is beautifully turned.

Gold-foil outlining

Triple-bud pommel

White jade

Watered-steel blade

Floral pattern of rubies and emeralds inlaid with gold

HILT OF JADE AND RUBIES

This late-17th-century Mughal hilt, attached to a fine Damascus blade, is crafted of white jade and inlaid with a cloverleaf motif in gold, rubies and emeralds. The delicacy of the work is evident in the tiny emeralds mounted at the base of each cloverleaf. This hilt exemplifies how even the most refined Mughal hilts could be attached to superb blades that were extremely effective weapons.

INDO-PERSIAN CURVED DAGGER

Designed for everyday functions such as hunting and cutting, this curved dagger dates from the early 19th century. It utilizes an antelope horn for the handle, which has a natural ergonomic shape.

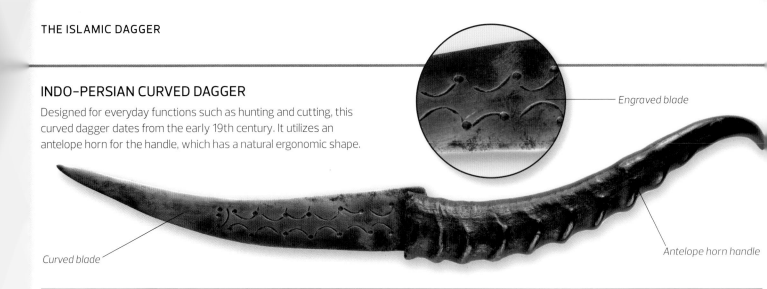

Engraved blade

Antelope horn handle

Curved blade

THREE-BLADE INDO-PERSIAN SPRING DAGGER

This rare and unusual Indo-Persian knife has a three-piece blade. While it appeared to be an ordinary knife to a sword-wielding attacker, the user separated the blades by means of a spring-loaded hinge in the hope of catching the attacker's sword blade between the main blade and one of the auxiliary blades. Twisting the knife would then immobilize (or, even better, break) the sword blade, allowing the defender to use his own sword on his opponent.

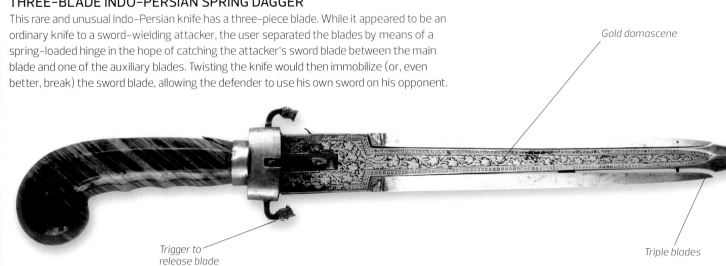

Gold damascene

Trigger to release blade

Triple blades

INDO-PERSIAN DAGGER WITH SHEATH

This is a late-19th-century classic straight and tapering Indo-Persian dagger, complete with brass sheath. The handle is decorated with brass and semiprecious stones.

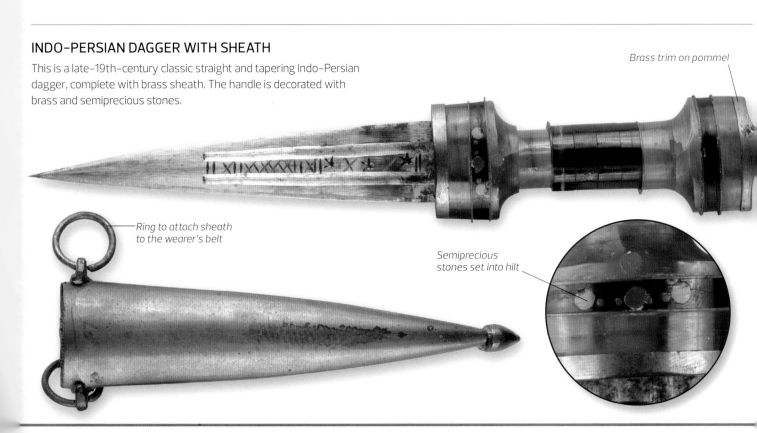

Brass trim on pommel

Ring to attach sheath to the wearer's belt

Semiprecious stones set into hilt

STRAIGHT-BLADED MUGHAL DAGGER AND SHEATH

A beautiful Mughal dagger with a straight, acute blade and a hilt of polished jade. The pistol-grip hilt is inlaid with floral designs in gold foil with rubies, emeralds, and diamonds; the wooden sheath, covered in velvet, also has fittings of precious stones and gold set in carved jade. The delicacy of the decorative work is extremely refined, as is the inlaid gold calligraphy at the base of the blade.

Rubies and emeralds form leaves and flowers

Trim on sheath matches hilt

Sheath of green velvet

INDO-PERSIAN BICHWA

The word *bichwa* means "sting of a scorpion," but the curved shape of this Indo-Persian example may have been inspired by a buffalo's horns. It has an open handle and curved blade. It dates from the mid-19th century.

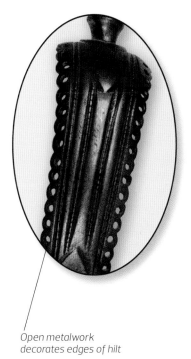

Narrow undulating blade

Open metalwork decorates edges of hilt

An 18th-century painting of a Mughal warrior and his wife shows him armed with pike, sword and dagger.

The Magnificence of Mughal Daggers

The daggers on view here represent the pinnacle of the Mughal knifemaker's art: Damascus blades with delicate inlays of arabesque patterns and stylized calligraphy, exquisitely carved and polished handles, refined inlays of precious materials, and a remarkable sense of form and balance to both eye and hand. With the possible exception of Japan, no other civilization has so completely and successfully aestheticized bladed weapons.

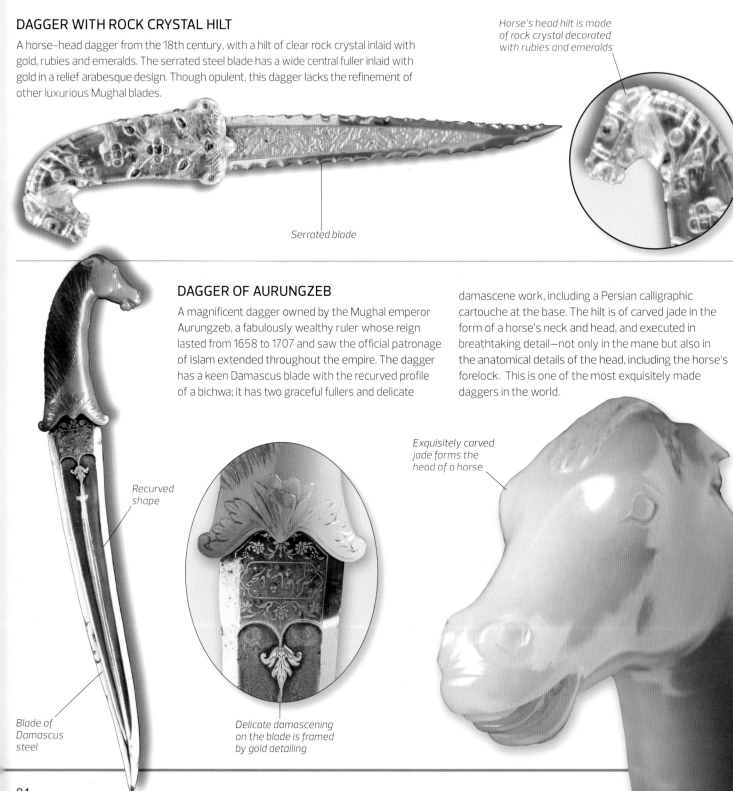

DAGGER WITH ROCK CRYSTAL HILT

A horse–head dagger from the 18th century, with a hilt of clear rock crystal inlaid with gold, rubies and emeralds. The serrated steel blade has a wide central fuller inlaid with gold in a relief arabesque design. Though opulent, this dagger lacks the refinement of other luxurious Mughal blades.

Horse's head hilt is made of rock crystal decorated with rubies and emeralds

Serrated blade

DAGGER OF AURUNGZEB

A magnificent dagger owned by the Mughal emperor Aurungzeb, a fabulously wealthy ruler whose reign lasted from 1658 to 1707 and saw the official patronage of Islam extended throughout the empire. The dagger has a keen Damascus blade with the recurved profile of a bichwa; it has two graceful fullers and delicate damascene work, including a Persian calligraphic cartouche at the base. The hilt is of carved jade in the form of a horse's neck and head, and executed in breathtaking detail—not only in the mane but also in the anatomical details of the head, including the horse's forelock. This is one of the most exquisitely made daggers in the world.

Recurved shape

Exquisitely carved jade forms the head of a horse

Blade of Damascus steel

Delicate damascening on the blade is framed by gold detailing

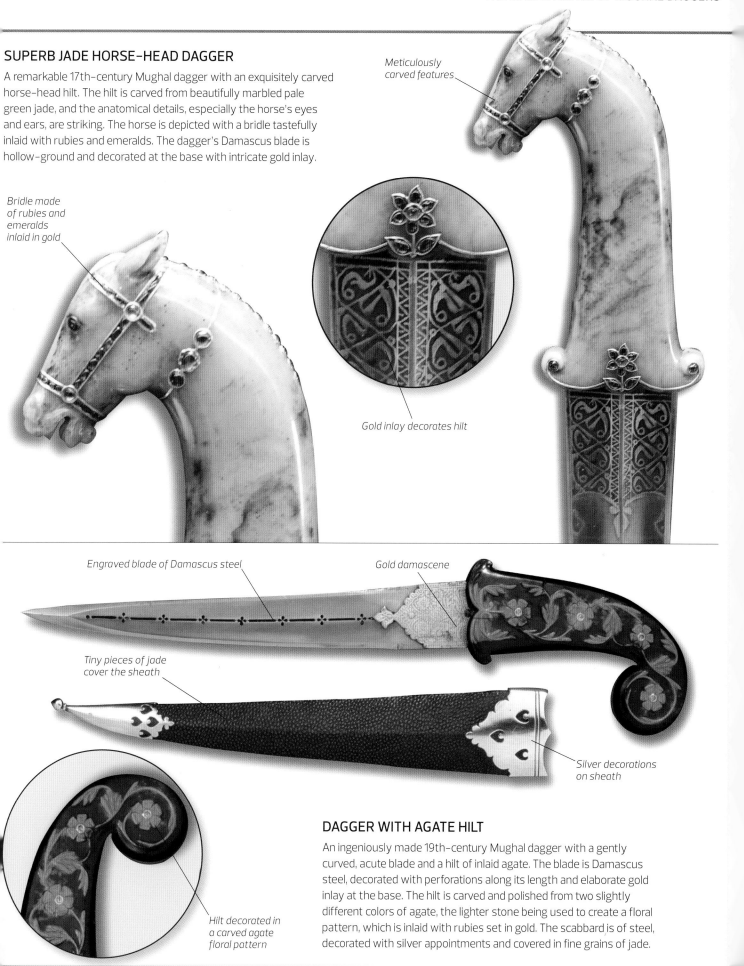

SUPERB JADE HORSE-HEAD DAGGER

A remarkable 17th-century Mughal dagger with an exquisitely carved horse-head hilt. The hilt is carved from beautifully marbled pale green jade, and the anatomical details, especially the horse's eyes and ears, are striking. The horse is depicted with a bridle tastefully inlaid with rubies and emeralds. The dagger's Damascus blade is hollow-ground and decorated at the base with intricate gold inlay.

Meticulously carved features

Bridle made of rubies and emeralds inlaid in gold

Gold inlay decorates hilt

Engraved blade of Damascus steel

Gold damascene

Tiny pieces of jade cover the sheath

Silver decorations on sheath

Hilt decorated in a carved agate floral pattern

DAGGER WITH AGATE HILT

An ingeniously made 19th-century Mughal dagger with a gently curved, acute blade and a hilt of inlaid agate. The blade is Damascus steel, decorated with perforations along its length and elaborate gold inlay at the base. The hilt is carved and polished from two slightly different colors of agate, the lighter stone being used to create a floral pattern, which is inlaid with rubies set in gold. The scabbard is of steel, decorated with silver appointments and covered in fine grains of jade.

Katara

The *katar* (plural *katara*) is the classic push dagger of the Indian subcontinent. Like the wootz steel that was used to form Damascus blades, it appears to have originated in the south, most likely in Tamil Nadu.

Its design is simple and effective: a double-edged triangular blade is mounted to an H-shaped hilt. The crossbar of the H serves as the grip, so that the base of the blade is in front of the knuckles, and the wielder literally punches with the blade. Katara rapidly became status symbols, and members of the warrior caste in particular took pride in the quality and workmanship of their blades.

Mughal warriors also made use of the katar. Not only did they use these knives for self-defense and combat, they also used them to hunt large game, including tigers. Using only the katar was considered the supreme test of courage and combat skill.

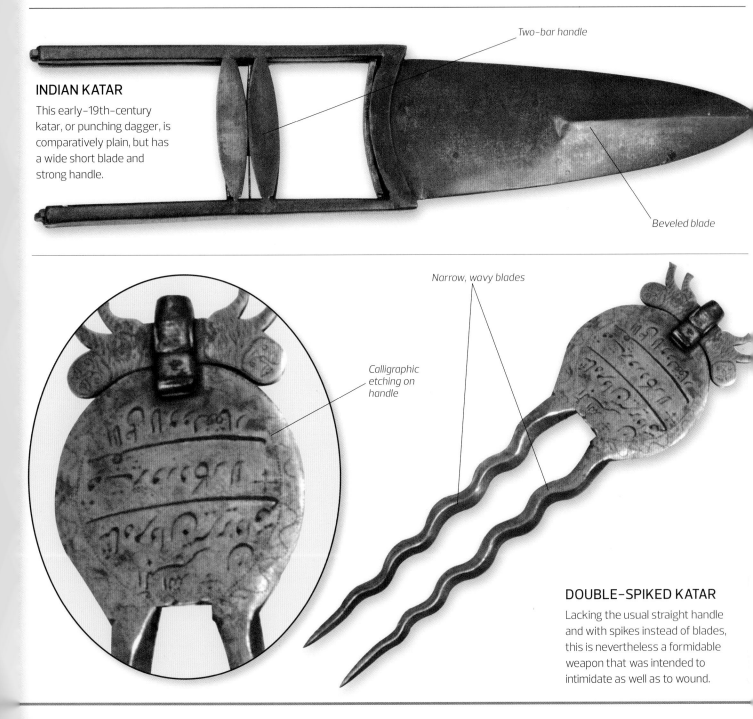

Two-bar handle

INDIAN KATAR

This early-19th-century katar, or punching dagger, is comparatively plain, but has a wide short blade and strong handle.

Beveled blade

Narrow, wavy blades

Calligraphic etching on handle

DOUBLE-SPIKED KATAR

Lacking the usual straight handle and with spikes instead of blades, this is nevertheless a formidable weapon that was intended to intimidate as well as to wound.

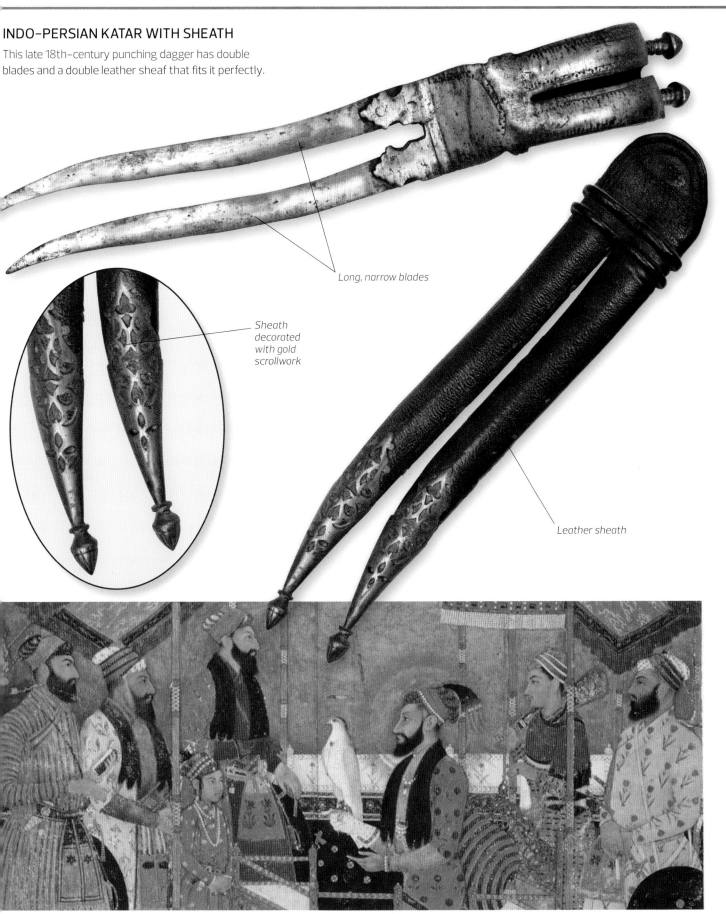

INDO-PERSIAN KATAR WITH SHEATH

This late 18th-century punching dagger has double blades and a double leather sheaf that fits it perfectly.

Long, narrow blades

Sheath decorated with gold scrollwork

Leather sheath

A scene from the court of Aurangzeb, the sixth Mughal emperor shows his courtiers with daggers at their waists, including a katar on the man second from left.

KATAR WITH TWO PISTOLS

Although similar to the other katara shown here, this lethal weapon also houses two percussion-cap pistols hidden within the spring-loaded handle. It was made in India in the 19th century.

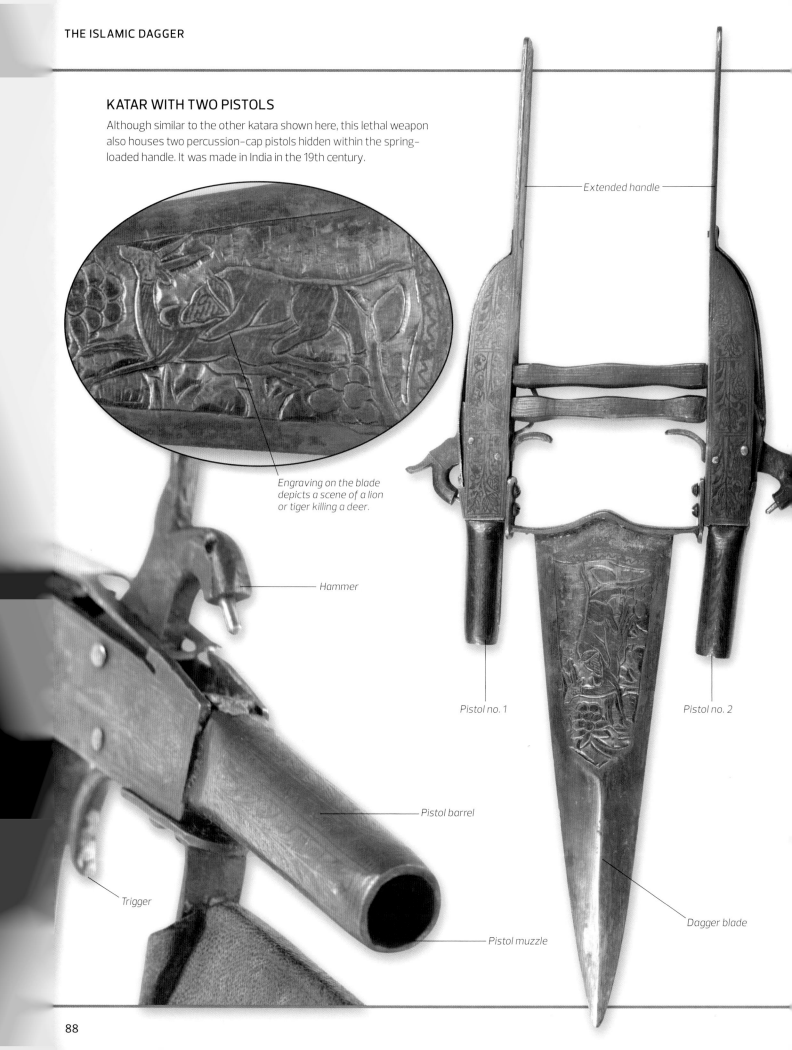

Extended handle

Engraving on the blade depicts a scene of a lion or tiger killing a deer.

Hammer

Pistol no. 1

Pistol no. 2

Pistol barrel

Trigger

Dagger blade

Pistol muzzle

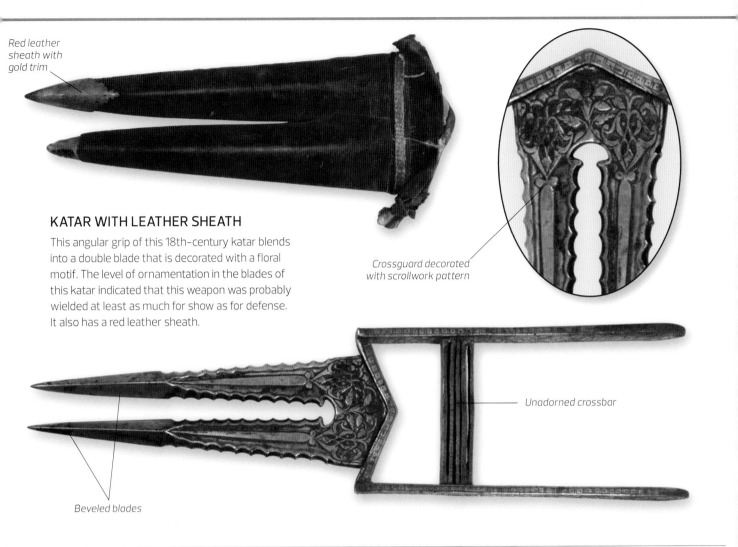

Red leather sheath with gold trim

KATAR WITH LEATHER SHEATH

This angular grip of this 18th-century katar blends into a double blade that is decorated with a floral motif. The level of ornamentation in the blades of this katar indicated that this weapon was probably wielded at least as much for show as for defense. It also has a red leather sheath.

Crossguard decorated with scrollwork pattern

Unadorned crossbar

Beveled blades

INDIAN KATAR WITH HAND GUARD

This dagger, dating to the 19th century, has the traditional katar handle supplemented by a triangular hand guard. The guard was added later to protect the user's hand from his opponent's blade.

Curved metal "hilt" to protect the user's hand

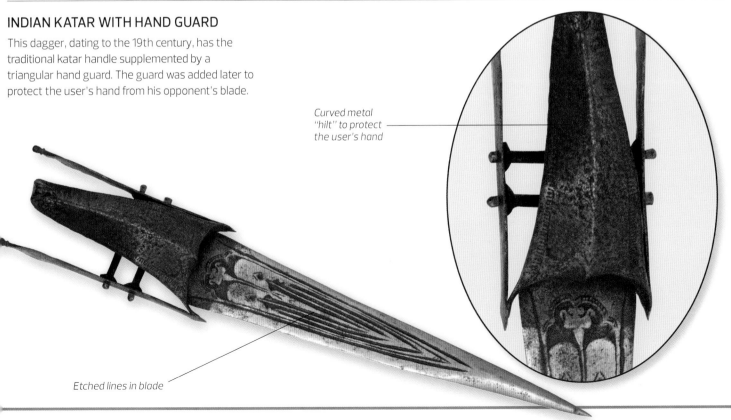

Etched lines in blade

Other Islamic and Indic Daggers

Various styles of dagger developed in Central and South Asia, many of them designed for specific combat situations. One such knife is the *pesh kabz*, which originated in Persia but spread widely due to its effective, purpose-specific design.

The pesh kabz is constructed to pierce chain mail; its hollow-ground blade narrows to a stiff triangular point that could penetrate a link in the mail and allow the rest of the blade to slip through.

Also widely used was the bichwa, named because of its recurved blade's resemblance to a scorpion's tail. The name was particularly apt given how easily a bichwa could be concealed for treacherous use.

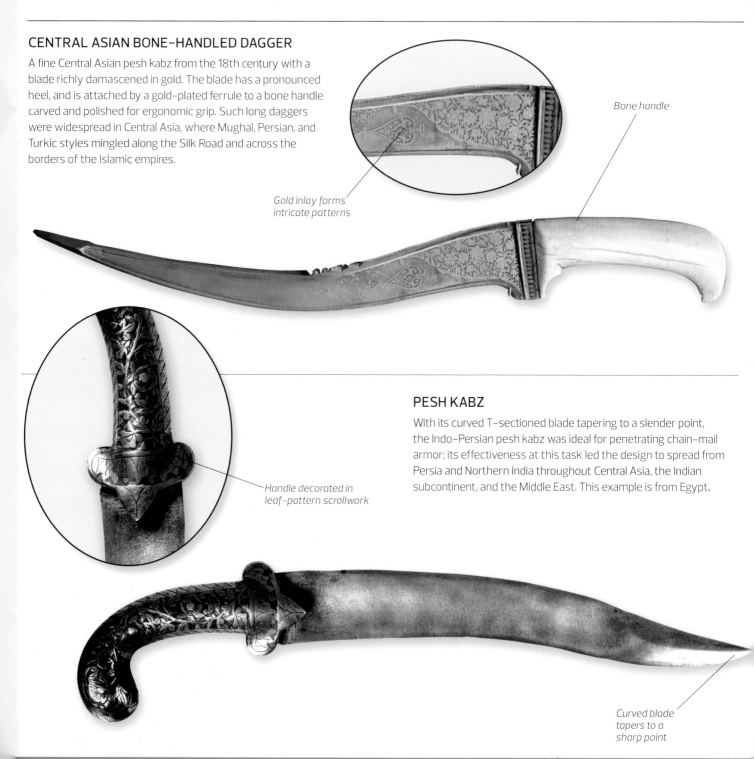

CENTRAL ASIAN BONE-HANDLED DAGGER

A fine Central Asian pesh kabz from the 18th century with a blade richly damascened in gold. The blade has a pronounced heel, and is attached by a gold-plated ferrule to a bone handle carved and polished for ergonomic grip. Such long daggers were widespread in Central Asia, where Mughal, Persian, and Turkic styles mingled along the Silk Road and across the borders of the Islamic empires.

Bone handle

Gold inlay forms intricate patterns

Handle decorated in leaf-pattern scrollwork

PESH KABZ

With its curved T-sectioned blade tapering to a slender point, the Indo-Persian pesh kabz was ideal for penetrating chain-mail armor; its effectiveness at this task led the design to spread from Persia and Northern India throughout Central Asia, the Indian subcontinent, and the Middle East. This example is from Egypt.

Curved blade tapers to a sharp point

INDIAN DAGGER

This early-19th-century dagger comes from India. It has superb elegant and restrained engraving work on both the sheath and the handle.

Delicate engraving

Asymmetrical quillons

INDIAN BICHWA DAGGER

Made in India in the late 19th century, this dagger has an interesting open metalwork handle and curved blade.

Subtle gold details on base of blade

Slender, tapering blade

Curved metal handle

AFGHAN PESH KABZ

This 18th-century pesh kabz, with a blade tapering to a slender point, was made in Afghanistan. It features a ivory handle and gold inlay on the blade.

Ivory handle

Gold inlay

Islamic Axes and Maces

Though Islamic cultures have venerable traditions of the sword and knife, axes were also prominent in the Mughal, Persian and Ottoman armories. In keeping with these cultures' richly aesthetic approach to weapons manufacture, their axes are also often things of beauty; many are made with stylized blades and engraved with intricate arabesque designs and calligraphic cartouches.

Islamic maces vary little in form and function from those in Europe. They served as symbols of rank or command and were effective weapons against heavily armored opponents. Most surviving Islamic maces are remarkable durable, with both shafts and heads of steel. The heads of these maces are often flanged for maximum force at the point of impact, and both heads and shafts are often incised with decorative patterns.

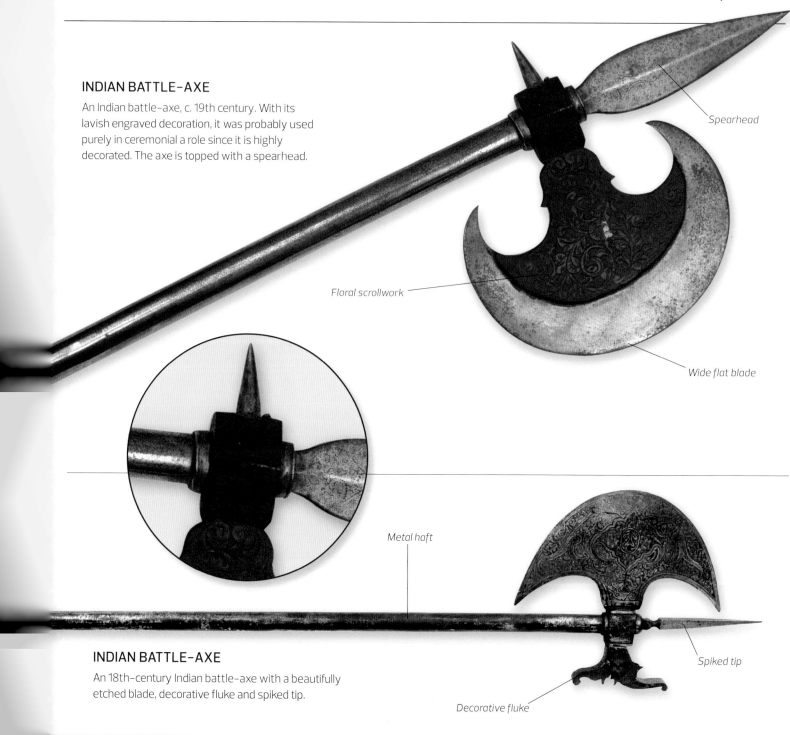

INDIAN BATTLE-AXE

An Indian battle-axe, c. 19th century. With its lavish engraved decoration, it was probably used purely in ceremonial a role since it is highly decorated. The axe is topped with a spearhead.

Spearhead

Floral scrollwork

Wide flat blade

Metal haft

Spiked tip

INDIAN BATTLE-AXE

An 18th-century Indian battle-axe with a beautifully etched blade, decorative fluke and spiked tip.

Decorative fluke

Copper finial

MUGHAL CEREMONIAL MACE

This impressive mace, made around 1600, is crafted from wood and overlaid with mother-of-pearl. Mother-of-pearl decoration was the speciality of Gujarati craftsmen, who used it here for both inlay and as scale-like paillettes over the mace's wooden base.

Extremely large and heavy, it was likely used only for ceremonial purposes. Maces of similar design appear in Mughal paintings, carried by court attendants; the weight of this on would probably meant that the attendant would have to carry it over his shoulder.

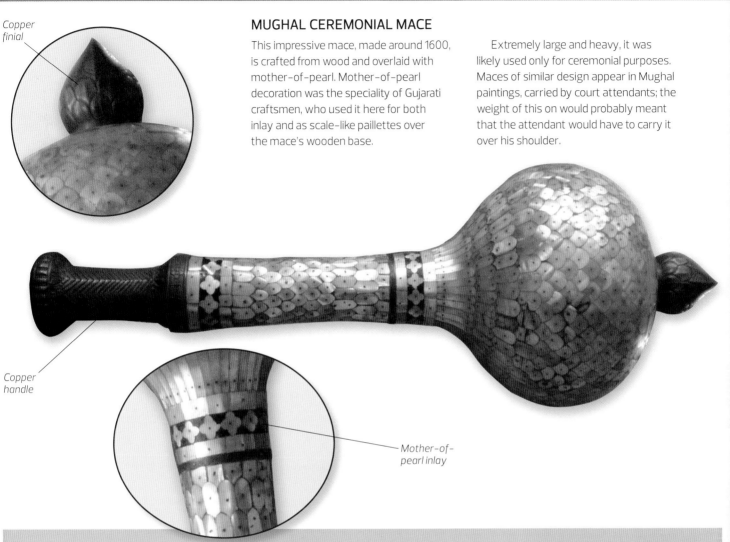

Copper handle

Mother-of-pearl inlay

GORZ

Among ancient weapons till extant today are a number of bull-headed maces/clubs. These maces, known as *gorz*, could be powerful weapons in real-life battle, but they are also described in many classical Persian texts dealing with mythical, religious and epic topics. In these, both divine entities and terrestrial figures wield the gorz as a symbol of the victory of justice over oppression and order over chaos.

An illustration from the 10th-century Persian epic *Rostam and Sohrab* shows Rostam striking a white elephant with an ox-headed mace.

Daggers of South and East Asia

Exquisite Blades of the East

While the Mughal Empire produced some of the finest daggers in history, other traditions in South and East Asia have their own extraordinary virtues. The often colorfully enameled mountings of Chinese daggers reflect that civilization's rich ceramics traditions. The ritual tantric daggers of Tibet are powerfully iconic instruments of spiritual practice, just as the kukri of Nepal is one of the most feared combat weapons on earth. The superb dagger blades of Japan, made of folded and differentially hardened steel in lethally elegant forms and fitted with exquisite mountings that are themselves treasured works of art, are some of the finest weapons ever made.

A 19TH-CENTURY WOODBLOCK print by Kuniyoshi Utagawa, showing the Japanese hero Minamoto Yorimitsu using a long *tanto* to battle a giant spider.

Chinese Daggers

As in many other countries, daggers have served as both weapon and ornament through the millennia of Chinese history. More expensive examples are lavished with the full repertoire of Chinese materials and decorative techniques, from intricate carving in ivory and jade to inlaid gemstones and colorfully enameled patterns. The enameling technique known as cloisonné, which arrived in China from the West around the 14th century, gave rise to vivid blade mountings in an array of colors, usually in classic decorative patterns.

ORNATE-HANDLED CHINESE KNIFE

This 17th-century Chinese knife has an exquisitely carved and shaped ceremonial dragon.

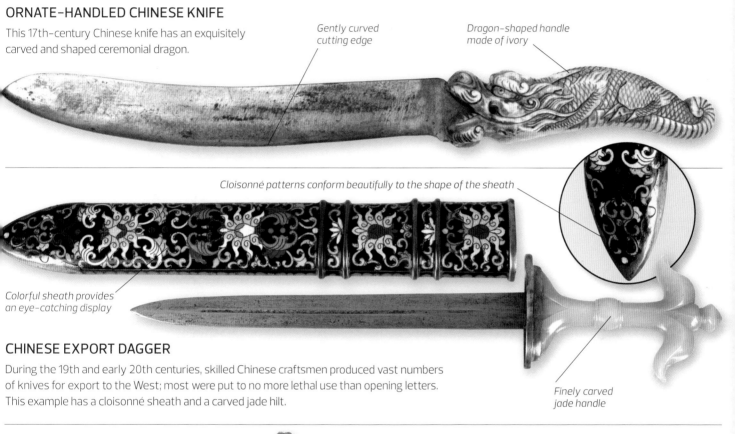

Gently curved cutting edge

Dragon-shaped handle made of ivory

Cloisonné patterns conform beautifully to the shape of the sheath

Colorful sheath provides an eye-catching display

CHINESE EXPORT DAGGER

During the 19th and early 20th centuries, skilled Chinese craftsmen produced vast numbers of knives for export to the West; most were put to no more lethal use than opening letters. This example has a cloisonné sheath and a carved jade hilt.

Finely carved jade handle

CHINESE IMPERIAL DAGGER

The scabbard and hilt of this dagger are silver, decorated with filigree and inlaid with semiprecious stones. Daggers like these were used by palace guards and officers of the old Imperial Army in the early 1800s.

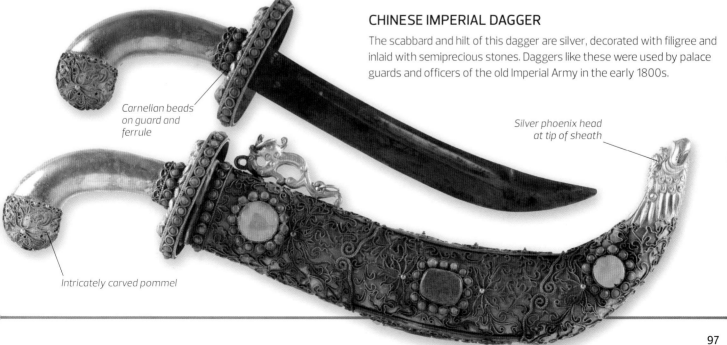

Carnelian beads on guard and ferrule

Silver phoenix head at tip of sheath

Intricately carved pommel

Intricately enameled floral pattern

Cloisonné enamel produces rich depth of color

Understated guard contrasts with cloisonné

CLOISONNÉ DAGGERS AND SHEATHS

Two examples of highly decorated knives and sheathes dating from the 19th century. Cloisonné enamel has been used on both the hilt and sheath.

Sheath presents a softened profile of the blade

Single fuller toward spine of blade

Striking contrasts of bright and dark color enhance visual appeal

Hilt and sheath form one continuous decorative pattern

Gently curved blade

19TH–CENTURY CLOISONNÉ DAGGER

This Chinese curved dagger dates from the 19th century: the hilt and sheath top are made of brass.

Brass scabbard mouth

Carved jade medallion
on sheath

Acute blade taper toward tip

FLORAL DESIGN

An intricately decorated Chinese dagger with cloisonné
enamel on both the hilt and sheath.

Jade inlay on
sheath

Deep red background
for brighter colors

ELEGANT DAGGER

Another variation of the
curved Chinese dagger
with intricately
decorated cloisonné enamel
on both the hilt and sheath.

Sturdy blade has fuller
and reinforced tip

Brass scabbard
mouth

Decorative pattern
centered on grip

Japanese Daggers

Japan boasts perhaps the finest blade-making tradition in the world. The traditional Japanese blade is a spiritual and artistic as well as martial object, and its construction of layered and differentially hardened steel is a laborious and highly ritualized process. The resulting blades have an unparalleled elegance of form and finish, and their every aspect, from tip profile to metal grain to the temper line shaped during the hardening and tempering processes, is appreciated for its aesthetic value, which is ultimately inseparable from the spirit behind and within the blade. The *tanto*, or dagger, was originally a sidearm used by samurai during the Heian Period (794–1185) and shortly after; if period accounts serve to indicate, it was mostly used for the taking of slain enemies' heads. Though it was gradually replaced in the samurai armory by the longer *wakizashi*, the tanto remained an important weapon, and some famed smiths specialized in tanto blades.

IVORY TANTO

A 19th-century tanto, this one with a hilt and sheath of intricately carved ivory depicting dragons—a popular motif.

Rounded and carved scabbard tip

Guard (tsuba) is also carved ivory

Dragon's head has inlaid eyes

TANTO

This 19th-century example of the tanto, or Japanese dagger, has a dragon's head carved into the hilt. While often carried by samurai, the tanto later became identified with the modern *yakuza*, criminal gangs that (though this is subject to debate) have existed in various forms in Japan for centuries.

Intricate ceremonial dragon design

Traditional decorative motifs carved in scabbard

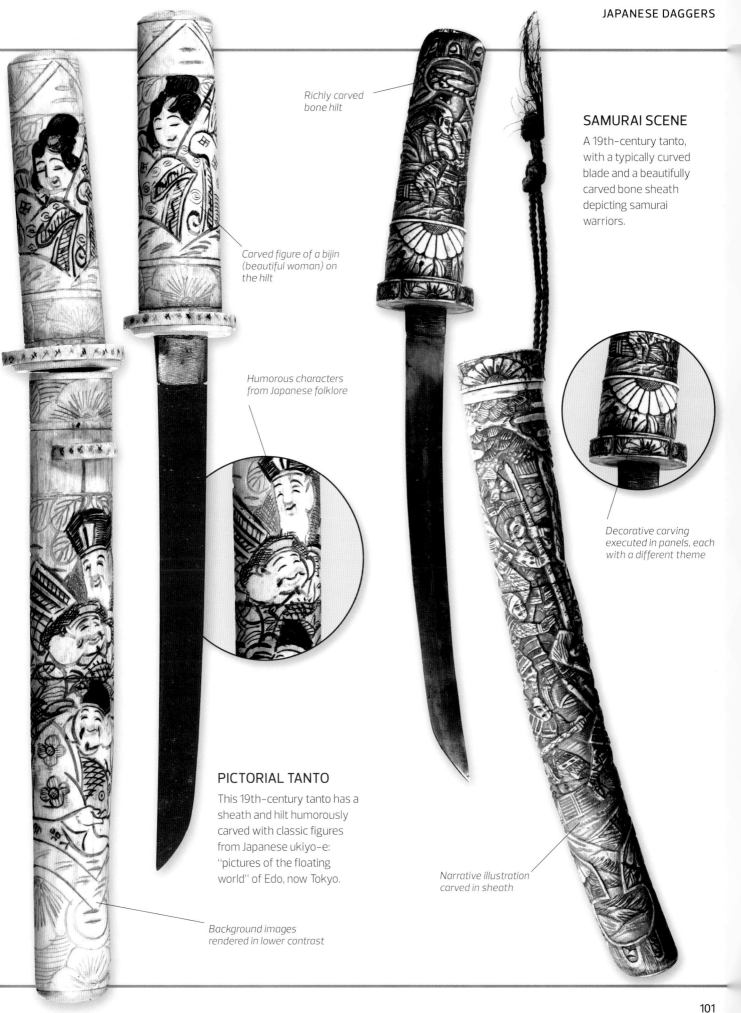

Richly carved
bone hilt

SAMURAI SCENE

A 19th-century tanto,
with a typically curved
blade and a beautifully
carved bone sheath
depicting samurai
warriors.

Carved figure of a bijin
(beautiful woman) on
the hilt

Humorous characters
from Japanese folklore

Decorative carving
executed in panels, each
with a different theme

PICTORIAL TANTO

This 19th-century tanto has a
sheath and hilt humorously
carved with classic figures
from Japanese ukiyo-e:
"pictures of the floating
world" of Edo, now Tokyo.

Narrative illustration
carved in sheath

Background images
rendered in lower contrast

Japanese Blade Mountings

The Japanese reverence for swords and other bladed weapons led to their being mounted with exquisitely crafted and decorated hilts and scabbards. These mountings, or *koshirae*, feature not only detailed carving and gilding, but also delicate work in *urushi*, or natural lacquer. *Maki-e*, combining polished lacquer with brushwork and inlays of gold and other materials, such as abalone, has produced some of the most refined artistry ever seen in weapons— or elsewhere. Every part of the mounting, from the heel of the grip to the butt end of the scabbard, is used as a decorative surface, and mountings are often composed around artistic themes. Matching sets of sword and dagger mountings are also commons. Like the blades themselves, superb mountings have been passed down through generations of owners, and some have become national treasures.

Rice grains of
inlaid abalone

Silk tassel on
hanging cord

DECORATIVE TANTO MOUNTING
An exquisite 18th-century Edo-period tanto mounting decorated with motifs of birds amid rice fields. The quail and duck are finely carved in gilded copper, and mounted on a wooden sheath decorated with maki-e (gold painting with urushi lacquer). The rice grains are rendered with inlaid bits of abalone. Refined mountings such as this are an essential part of the Japanese aesthetic of bladed weapons.

Gold quail with
its eggs

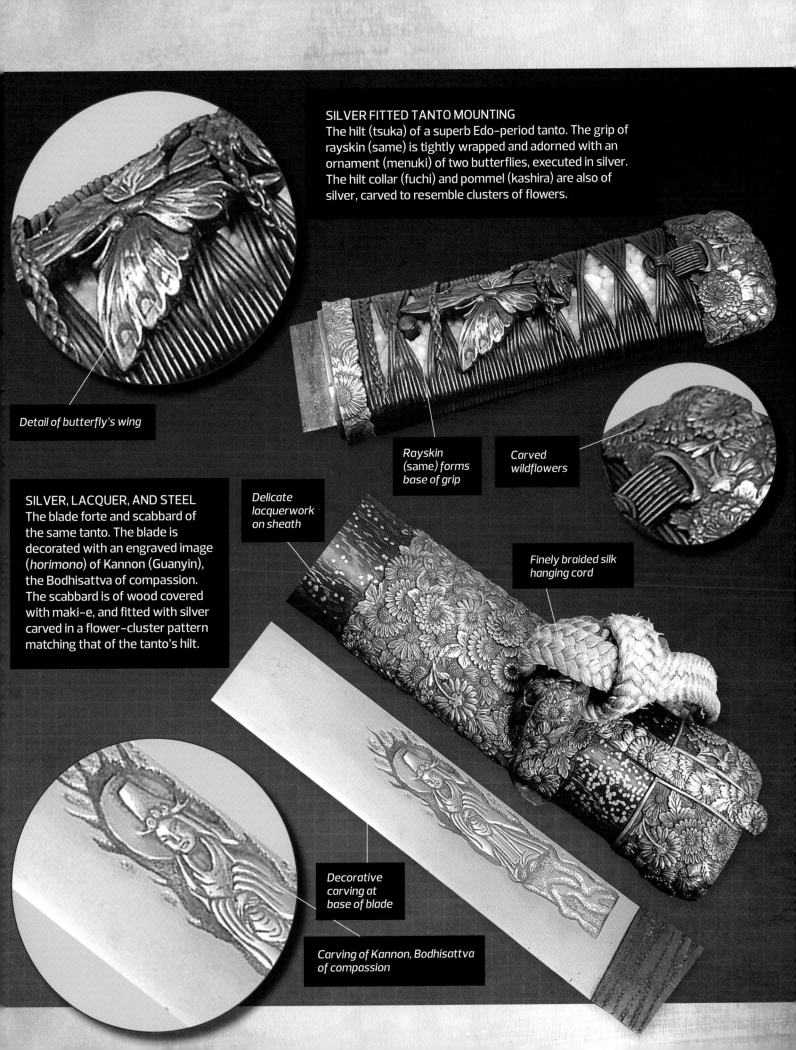

SILVER FITTED TANTO MOUNTING
The hilt (tsuka) of a superb Edo-period tanto. The grip of rayskin (same) is tightly wrapped and adorned with an ornament (menuki) of two butterflies, executed in silver. The hilt collar (fuchi) and pommel (kashira) are also of silver, carved to resemble clusters of flowers.

Detail of butterfly's wing

Rayskin (same) forms base of grip

Carved wildflowers

SILVER, LACQUER, AND STEEL
The blade forte and scabbard of the same tanto. The blade is decorated with an engraved image (*horimono*) of Kannon (Guanyin), the Bodhisattva of compassion. The scabbard is of wood covered with maki–e, and fitted with silver carved in a flower–cluster pattern matching that of the tanto's hilt.

Delicate lacquerwork on sheath

Finely braided silk hanging cord

Decorative carving at base of blade

Carving of Kannon, Bodhisattva of compassion

Himalayan Daggers

Among the most instantly recognizable daggers in the world is the ritual dagger of Tibetan tantric traditions: the *phurba*. Indian in origin—phurba being a Tibetan rendering of the Sanskrit *kīla*, the word for "spike"—the phurba likely originated as a simple peg for tying down tents. According to Tibetan Buddhist lore, Padmasambhava, the monk who brought Vajrayana Buddhism to Tibet in the 8th century, established the site of the Samye temple by stabbing such a peg into the earth on the site.

Ritually, the phuba functions as both a blade and a spike. As the former, it cuts the bonds that tie tantric practitioners to the wheel of limited existence; as the latter, it can be used to pin down and bind evil spirits, or the forces of ignorance and delusion in the psyche. The pommel end can be used to confer blessings. The iconography of the phurba's various segments is highly specific. Other Tibetan ritual daggers, such as the flaying blade and the scorpion knife, are made for similar ends.

ORNATE TIBETAN PHURBA

A beautifully fashioned phurba from the 16th century. The triple-edged iron spike is mounted to a hilt of silver and gold. The spike itself is adorned with silver twined snakes, associated with spiritual energy in Tantric traditions. Above the spike is a gold-plated makara, a mythical aquatic beast; a vajra, or thunderbolt, with knots of immutability at either end; and the gold-plated faces of three wrathful deities who subdue the poisons of ignorance, desire, and hate. The pommel is capped with a small vajra, which can be used to dispense blessings.

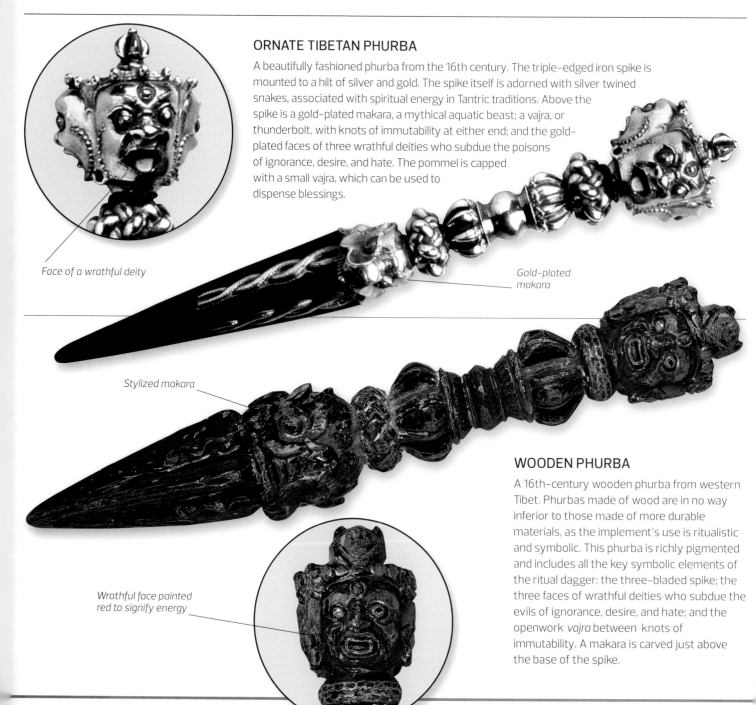

Face of a wrathful deity

Gold-plated makara

Stylized makara

WOODEN PHURBA

A 16th-century wooden phurba from western Tibet. Phurbas made of wood are in no way inferior to those made of more durable materials, as the implement's use is ritualistic and symbolic. This phurba is richly pigmented and includes all the key symbolic elements of the ritual dagger: the three-bladed spike; the three faces of wrathful deities who subdue the evils of ignorance, desire, and hate; and the openwork *vajra* between knots of immutability. A makara is carved just above the base of the spike.

Wrathful face painted red to signify energy

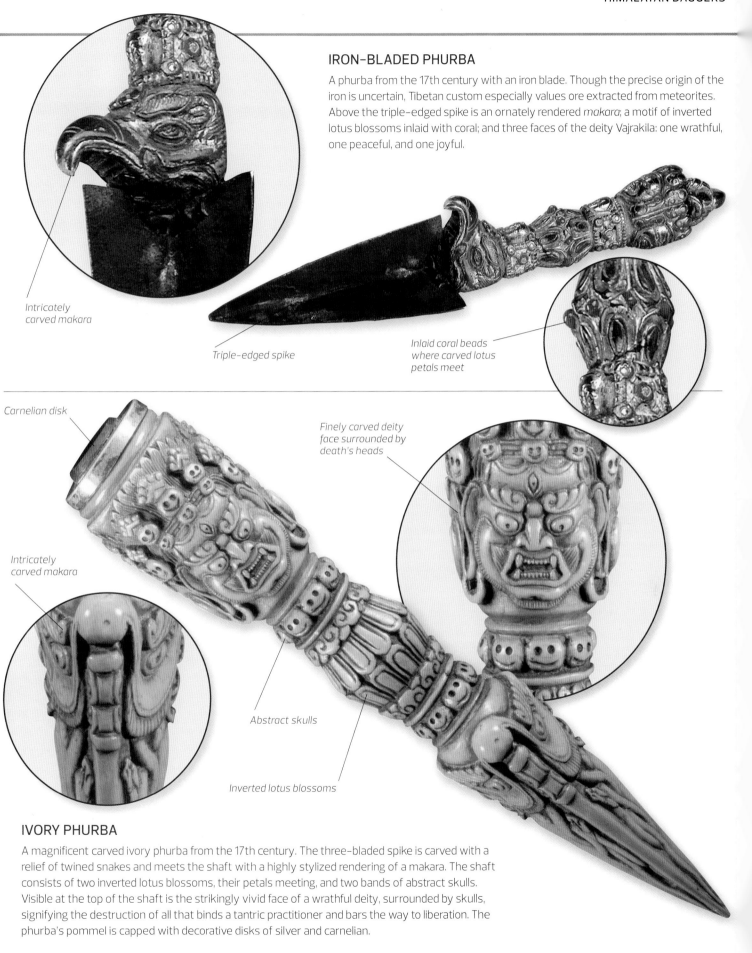

IRON-BLADED PHURBA

A phurba from the 17th century with an iron blade. Though the precise origin of the iron is uncertain, Tibetan custom especially values ore extracted from meteorites. Above the triple-edged spike is an ornately rendered *makara*; a motif of inverted lotus blossoms inlaid with coral; and three faces of the deity Vajrakila: one wrathful, one peaceful, and one joyful.

Intricately carved makara

Triple-edged spike

Inlaid coral beads where carved lotus petals meet

Carnelian disk

Finely carved deity face surrounded by death's heads

Intricately carved makara

Abstract skulls

Inverted lotus blossoms

IVORY PHURBA

A magnificent carved ivory phurba from the 17th century. The three-bladed spike is carved with a relief of twined snakes and meets the shaft with a highly stylized rendering of a makara. The shaft consists of two inverted lotus blossoms, their petals meeting, and two bands of abstract skulls. Visible at the top of the shaft is the strikingly vivid face of a wrathful deity, surrounded by skulls, signifying the destruction of all that binds a tantric practitioner and bars the way to liberation. The phurba's pommel is capped with decorative disks of silver and carnelian.

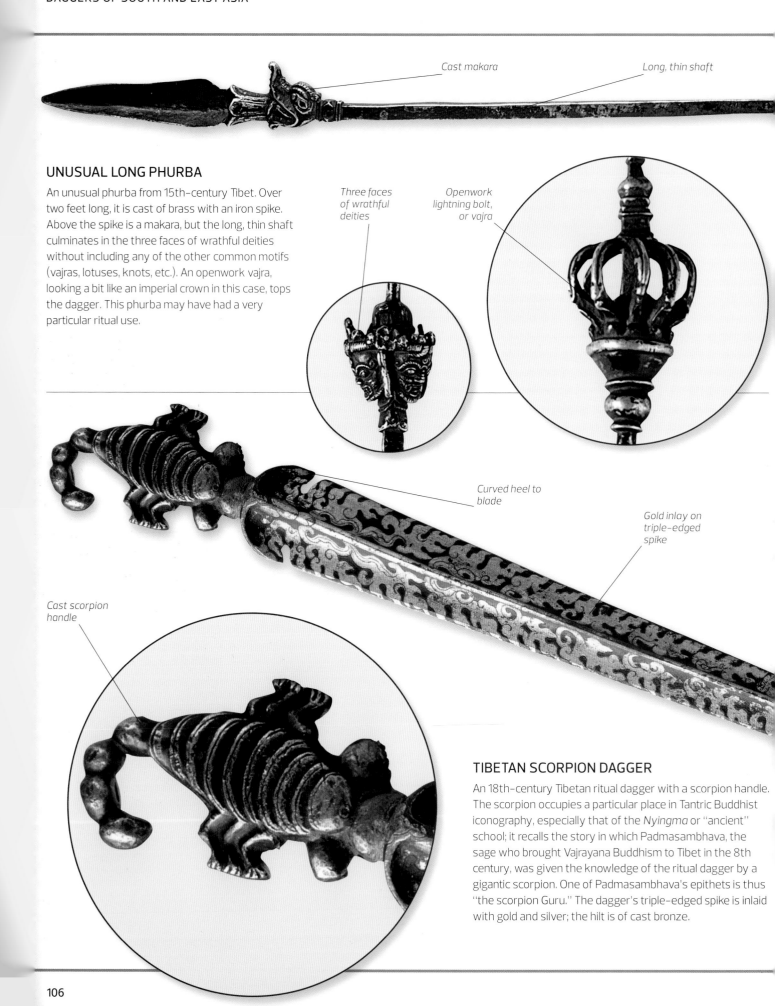

Cast makara

Long, thin shaft

UNUSUAL LONG PHURBA

An unusual phurba from 15th–century Tibet. Over two feet long, it is cast of brass with an iron spike. Above the spike is a makara, but the long, thin shaft culminates in the three faces of wrathful deities without including any of the other common motifs (vajras, lotuses, knots, etc.). An openwork vajra, looking a bit like an imperial crown in this case, tops the dagger. This phurba may have had a very particular ritual use.

Three faces of wrathful deities

Openwork lightning bolt, or vajra

Curved heel to blade

Gold inlay on triple–edged spike

Cast scorpion handle

TIBETAN SCORPION DAGGER

An 18th–century Tibetan ritual dagger with a scorpion handle. The scorpion occupies a particular place in Tantric Buddhist iconography, especially that of the *Nyingma* or "ancient" school; it recalls the story in which Padmasambhava, the sage who brought Vajrayana Buddhism to Tibet in the 8th century, was given the knowledge of the ritual dagger by a gigantic scorpion. One of Padmasambhava's epithets is thus "the scorpion Guru." The dagger's triple–edged spike is inlaid with gold and silver; the hilt is of cast bronze.

Knot motif near pommel

ROCK CRYSTAL PHURBA

A rather primitively fashioned phurba from East Tibet, dating to the 17th century or earlier. Its spike is a triangular piece of rock crystal, fitted to the shaft with a gilded copper ferrule adorned with skulls. The shaft includes a makara, knots, two inverted lotuses, and a finial that may represent a vajra.

Detailed carving of makara

Makara head symbolically transfers energy into the blade

Rock crystal spike

TIBETAN RITUAL FLAYING KNIFE

An East Tibetan ritual flaying knife of rock crystal, made as a complementary implement to the rock crystal phurba shown on this page. The curved blade is modeled on Indian butchers' traditional flaying blades, and represents the power to cut through ignorance—or to flay the enemies of the Buddhist dharma. The rock crystal blade is fitted to the shaft with a ferrule decorated, like that of the phurba, with human skulls, above which the carved head of a makara seems to bite the blade. The pommel takes the form of a large vajra, emerging in customary fashion from a lotus blossom.

Classic shape of butcher's flaying blade

The Kukri

The Nepalese Gurkhas are renowned for their tremendous courage and skill, and are among the most feared and respected soldiers in the world. The famous Indian Field Marshal Sam Manekshaw (1914–2008) famously remarked, "If a man says he is not afraid of dying, he is either lying or a Gurkha." Their signature blade is the *kukri*, which is the national weapon of Nepal. Extremely well-balanced and devastatingly effective, the kukri has a single-edged blade angled sharply inward, ideal for hacking blows. The smiths who make these blades are a distinct caste in Nepalese culture. Around the world, the kukri remains one of the few truly iconic weapons, symbolic of bravery and loyalty.

PRESENTATION KUKRI

An exquisite presentation kukri from 1819. Its hilt, with its characteristic flared pommel, is made of horn. The scabbard is adorned with ornate metalwork.

Flared, ergonomic pommel

Intricate openwork on scabbard

Classic angled blade

Presentation plaque

HORN-HANDLED KUKRI

A presentation kukri with a horn handle. The plaque on the plain-leather scabbard reads "From the Officers 2nd Battalion 5th Gurkha Rifles."

Carved and polished horn handle

Laces for adjusting tightness of sheath

Simply decorated, bone hilt

Regimental emblem set on sheath

Decorative inlay in hilt

REGIMENTAL KUKRI

A 19th-century regimental kukri. The distinctive leather sheath is adorned with a regimental emblem and holds a small utility knife.

Small utility knife

Ivory section of handle

Classic double notch at base of blade

Utility/sharpening knives

GURKHA KUKRI

A large kukri used in World War I by a member of the 9th Gurkha Rifles. Kukris were devastatingly effective weapons, reputedly capable of decapitating an opponent with a single blow.

Asian Axes

South, Southeast, and Central Asia all have weapons traditions that predated or developed largely outside the empires that stamped the cultures of those regions. The weapons of these cultures certainly resemble those of their later or larger neighbors, but they often have distinct decorative elements that mark them as the products of their cultures. These axes are all both instantly recognizable and distinctive.

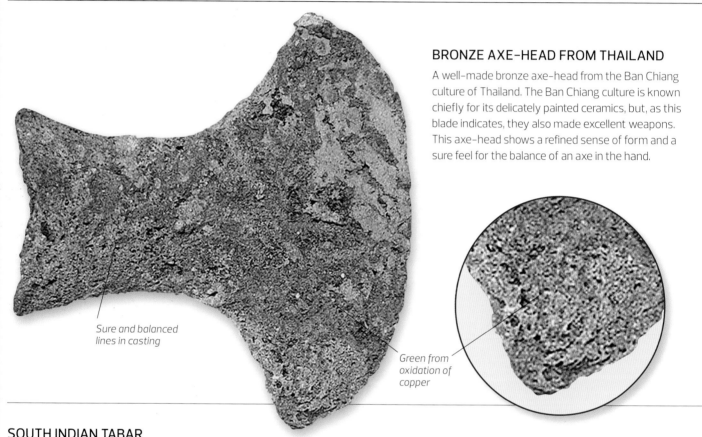

BRONZE AXE-HEAD FROM THAILAND

A well-made bronze axe-head from the Ban Chiang culture of Thailand. The Ban Chiang culture is known chiefly for its delicately painted ceramics, but, as this blade indicates, they also made excellent weapons. This axe-head shows a refined sense of form and a sure feel for the balance of an axe in the hand.

Sure and balanced lines in casting

Green from oxidation of copper

SOUTH INDIAN TABAR

A *tabar*, or battle-axe, from South India. This weapon is far more durable than it may seem; it has a solid tang that runs through most of the length of its wooden shaft, to which it is fixed by four rivets. The blade has a temper line from differential hardening, and is constructed to strike with a concentrated cleaving impact. Tabars were not only battlefield weapons; they also were carried by some religious renunciates as a sign of their spiritual commitment.

Rivets secure long tang to shaft

Brass butt end of shaft

Small but effective axe-head

TABAR-SHASHPAR

A rare example of a two-ended, dual-purpose weapon, this 18th-century *tabar-shashpar* (axe-mace) from the Deccan is Mughal in style.

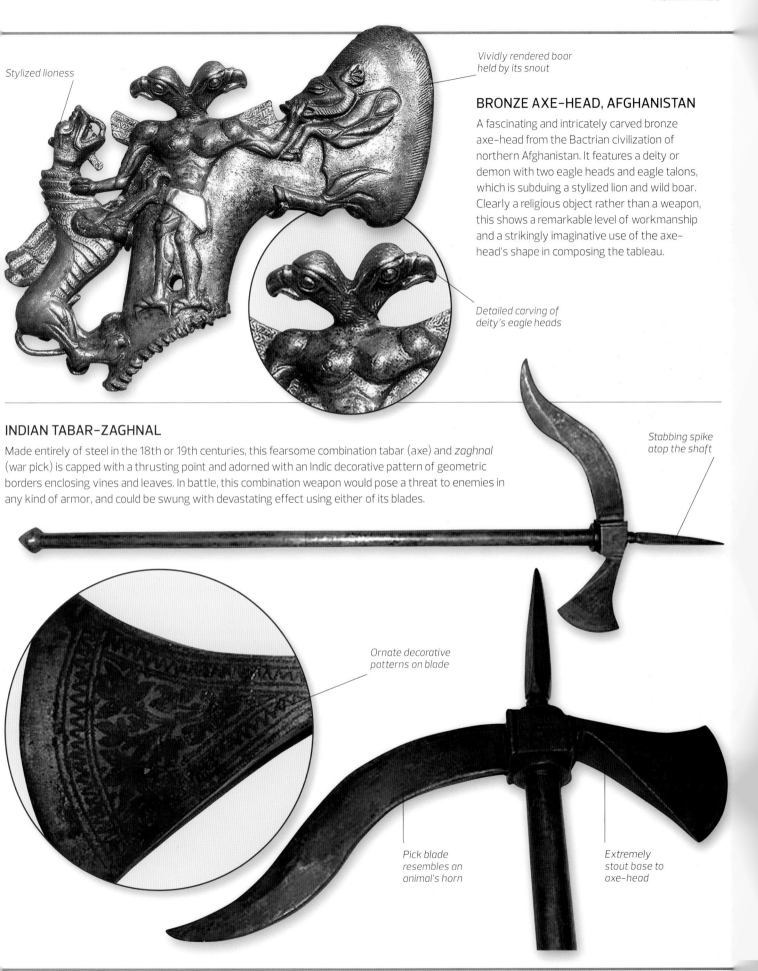

Stylized lioness

Vividly rendered boar held by its snout

BRONZE AXE-HEAD, AFGHANISTAN

A fascinating and intricately carved bronze axe-head from the Bactrian civilization of northern Afghanistan. It features a deity or demon with two eagle heads and eagle talons, which is subduing a stylized lion and wild boar. Clearly a religious object rather than a weapon, this shows a remarkable level of workmanship and a strikingly imaginative use of the axe-head's shape in composing the tableau.

Detailed carving of deity's eagle heads

INDIAN TABAR-ZAGHNAL

Made entirely of steel in the 18th or 19th centuries, this fearsome combination tabar (axe) and *zaghnal* (war pick) is capped with a thrusting point and adorned with an Indic decorative pattern of geometric borders enclosing vines and leaves. In battle, this combination weapon would pose a threat to enemies in any kind of armor, and could be swung with devastating effect using either of its blades.

Stabbing spike atop the shaft

Ornate decorative patterns on blade

Pick blade resembles an animal's horn

Extremely stout base to axe-head

A Wide World of Daggers

A 16TH- or 17th-century Nigerian plaque showing two warriors protecting the Yoruban king, whose left hand rests on a fighting knife tucked in his belt.

A Universal Weapon

The knife is a universal weapon and tool, and every culture has some tradition of knife-making. Many of these traditions have produced renowned and highly sought-after weapons, such as the *kriss* of Indonesia. The fighting knives of sub-Saharan Africa display an astonishing and inventive variety of blade shapes, and the ritual knives of the great Pre-Columbian civilizations are powerfully evocative. The dagger and other hand weapons can be seen in countless variations in this tour of global weapons traditions.

African Daggers

Sub-Saharan Africa has a vast and varied array of knife-making traditions. Perhaps nowhere else in the world has the knife blade been subjected to so many ingenious and dramatic designs, or used so strikingly as a symbol of rank or affluence. Many African fighting knives were adapted from agricultural implements, but others are obviously—and effectively—crafted solely for the purpose of combat. Some of the more stylized blades served ritual purposes, but they also might strike fear into the hearts of their wielders' adversaries. This is a fascinating collection of visually and technically impressive weapons.

Fur wrap on grip

Carved pommel with ivory pin functioning like a rivet.

WOODEN AFRICAN DAGGER

An example of a 20th-century African wooden dagger with a fur-covered handle.

Acute, crudely sharpened blade

AFRICAN RITUAL KNIFE

This African knife, probably made early in the 20th century, was used in ceremonial rituals. Its hilt is decorated with a tuft of animal hair.

Tapered ebony handle

Elegant blade ends in an acute stabbing point

AFRICAN FIGHTING KNIVES

This pair of North African fighting knives have ebony handles.

Hourglass-shaped hilt

Sickle-shaped blade ends

CONGO KNIFE

A wicked-looking long knife from the Konda or Mongo peoples of the Congo region. The long, broad, double-edged blade separates at its tip into four acute curves with sharpened inner edges. The tips would maximize the damage inflicted by a slashing attack, cutting deeply into an opponent during retraction as well as during the initial strike. The wooden handle is simple but ergonomically designed for a sure grip.

SAKA AFRICAN DAGGER

A large fighting knife of the Saka people of the Congo region. The eight-inch leaf-shaped blade is double-edged; in an interesting touch the tang extends out from the hilt to form a serrated utility blade behind the main blade. The hilt is of turned wood, the grip wrapped with copper ribbon and the substantial pommel adorned with metal studs.

Pommel flares at base of grip

Pommel can be used for striking

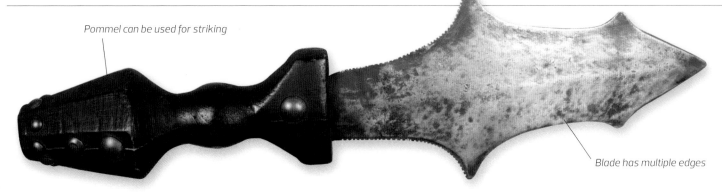

Blade has multiple edges

NKUTSHU DAGGER

A dagger of the Nkutshu people of Central Africa. The seven-inch blade features an array of edges: on each side of the blade a serrated curved edge, probably for utility, gives way to a smooth slicing edge, which then transitions into a moderately acute stabbing point. The substantial hilt is of one piece of wood, with a flared guard and a large faceted pommel adorned with metal studs and useful as a striking weapon.

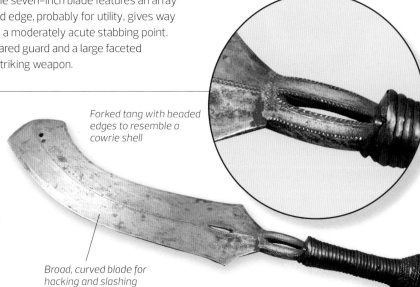

Forked tang with beaded edges to resemble a cowrie shell

NGBANDI KNIFE

A machete-like knife of the Ngbandi people of Central Africa. The broad blade is gently curved and double edged, so it is capable of delivering both slashing blows (with the outside edge) and shearing strokes (with the inside edge). The blade has a punched decoration in the forte, which echoes a two-pronged tang; both decorative elements resemble cowrie shells. The grip is wrapped in fiber and ends in a flared hilt wound with braided basketwork.

Broad, curved blade for hacking and slashing

NGBANDI FIGHTING BLADE

A long, sickle-bladed fighting knife of the Ngbandi people of Central Africa. The blade, stiffened with a central fuller, is sharpened on the inward edge and ends in an acute point. A small serrated portion of the tang extends from the handle, which is wrapped in plant fibers. Such a blade would have served both to clear brush and to deliver effective shearing blows in battle.

Grip wrapped in plant fiber

Ivory hilt with flared grip

MANGBETU TRUMBASH

A large sickle-bladed knife, or *trumbash*, from the Mangbetu people of Central Africa. The blade extends from a substantial heel through a forte decorated with punched holes and hooks, broadening significantly before turning a sharp curve. The inner edge is sharpened and the point acute, making this an effective weapon for both hacking and stabbing attacks. The handle is of ivory, flared at the pommel for secure grip.

Curved, sickle-like blade

Leaf-shaped blade

AFRICAN COPPER KNIFE

An African knife of unknown origin, featuring thick, leaf-shaped copper blade with no sharpened edges but an acute stabbing point. The handle is of ivory, carved with a series of cutouts for secure grip. This was clearly not designed for any utilitarian purpose; it was mostly made as a marker of its owner's status.

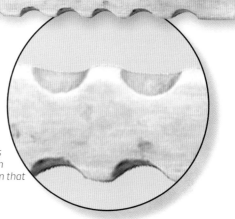

The evenly spaced cutouts in the ivory handle are both decorative and functional in that they offer secure grip

Integrated, acute blade

SONGYE KNIFE

An elegant knife of the Songye people of Central Africa. The weapon is forged from one piece of steel. The seven-inch blade is single-edged and tapers from an assertive heel to a very acute point. A continuous, very gentle curve extends into the round tang, which serves as a handle and ends in a figured pommel in the shape of a human head. An admirably balanced and effective blade.

The figured pommel of the Songye dagger. The human head is depicted as wearing a headband; it has the almond-shaped eyes and triangular nose that also characterize the famed masks of the Songye, a people renowned for their artwork.

Southeast Asian and Pacific Daggers

The various cultures of Southeast Asia, Indonesia, and the Pacific Islands have traditions of knife combat going back thousands of years. Some of these blades are linked to highly ritualized forms of combat, while others are variations on ordinary tools. From the most primitive bone thrusting weapons to the most finely balanced and appointed steel blades, these are traditionally constructed knives well suited to their purposes.

Stylized human face

NEW GUINEAN DAGGER

A one-piece dagger from Papua New Guinea, made from the bone of a Cassowary. The knife is effectively a stiletto, designed solely for thrusting attacks with its acute point. The end of the bone is left in its original form as a pommel, and the handle portion is carved with a highly stylized human face.

THREE NEW GUINEAN BONE KNIVES

Three New Guinean bone daggers. In these, the joint end of the bone is incorporated into the decorative work to varying extents. Two of the daggers are carved with serpentine motifs, stylized faces, and "eyes" that could house inlaid stones or beads. The third is carved all over with organic patterns, mostly of a spiral motif.

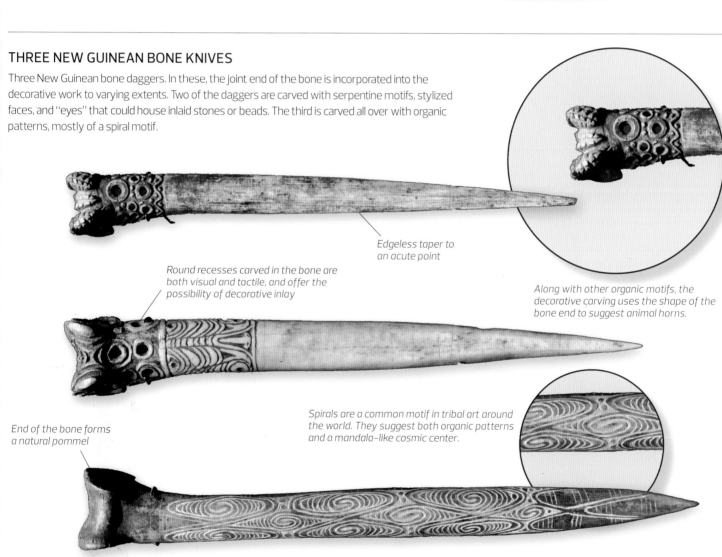

Edgeless taper to an acute point

Round recesses carved in the bone are both visual and tactile, and offer the possibility of decorative inlay

Along with other organic motifs, the decorative carving uses the shape of the bone end to suggest animal horns.

End of the bone forms a natural pommel

Spirals are a common motif in tribal art around the world. They suggest both organic patterns and a mandala-like cosmic center.

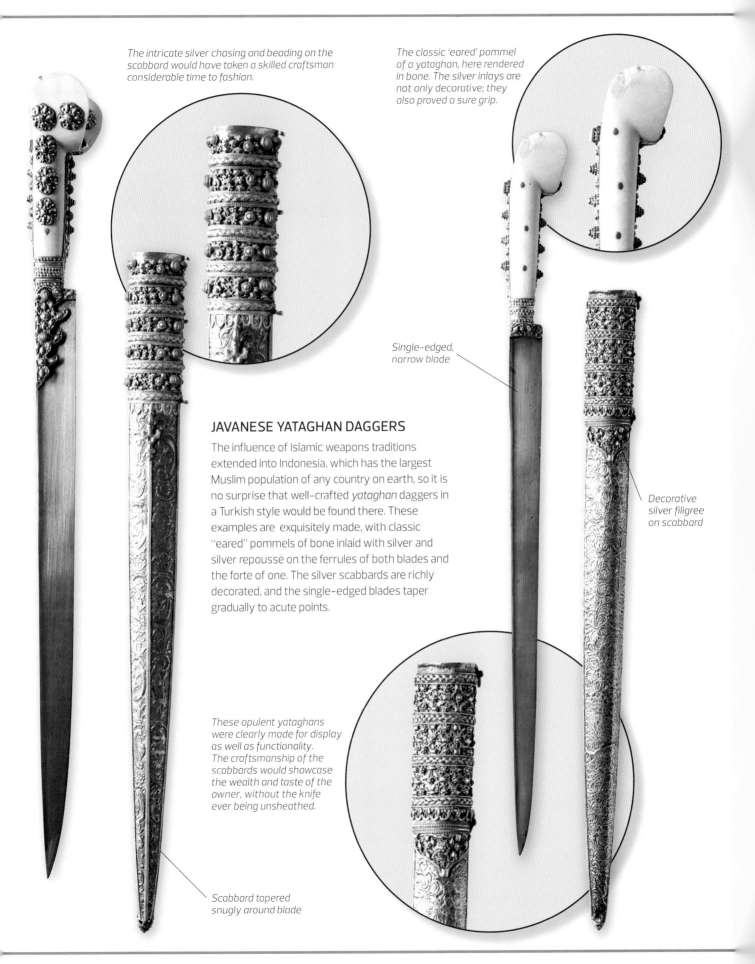

The intricate silver chasing and beading on the scabbard would have taken a skilled craftsman considerable time to fashion.

The classic 'eared' pommel of a yataghan, here rendered in bone. The silver inlays are not only decorative; they also proved a sure grip.

Single-edged, narrow blade

JAVANESE YATAGHAN DAGGERS

The influence of Islamic weapons traditions extended into Indonesia, which has the largest Muslim population of any country on earth, so it is no surprise that well-crafted *yataghan* daggers in a Turkish style would be found there. These examples are exquisitely made, with classic "eared" pommels of bone inlaid with silver and silver repoussé on the ferrules of both blades and the forte of one. The silver scabbards are richly decorated, and the single-edged blades taper gradually to acute points.

Decorative silver filigree on scabbard

These opulent yataghans were clearly made for display as well as functionality. The craftsmanship of the scabbards would showcase the wealth and taste of the owner, without the knife ever being unsheathed.

Scabbard tapered snugly around blade

JAVANESE PEDANG

A superb Javanese *pedang* dagger, made around 1850 and owned by Pakubuwono X (1866–1939), the tenth ruler of Surakarta in Java. The single-edged blade is gently curved and widens slightly before narrowing to a fairly acute point; it is decorated along its length with fine filigree. The pistol-shaped hilt is of carved and chased gold, including a short crossguard, and the gold-plated scabbard features fine repoussé work.

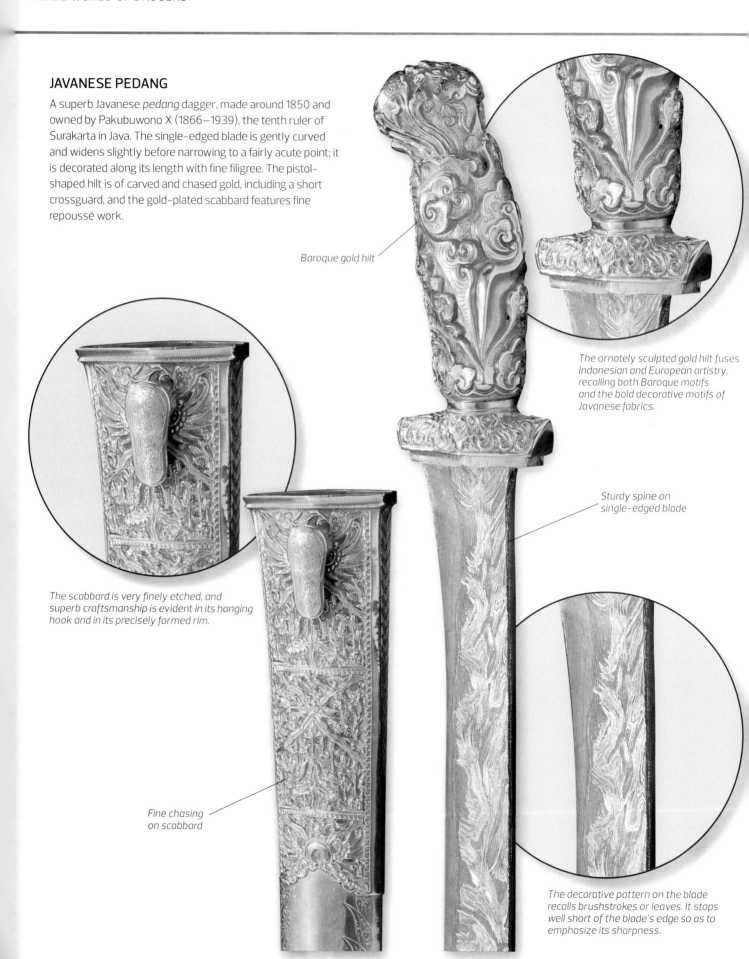

Baroque gold hilt

The ornately sculpted gold hilt fuses Indonesian and European artistry, recalling both Baroque motifs and the bold decorative motifs of Javanese fabrics.

The scabbard is very finely etched, and superb craftsmanship is evident in its hanging hook and in its precisely formed rim.

Fine chasing on scabbard

Sturdy spine on single-edged blade

The decorative pattern on the blade recalls brushstrokes or leaves. It stops well short of the blade's edge so as to emphasize its sharpness.

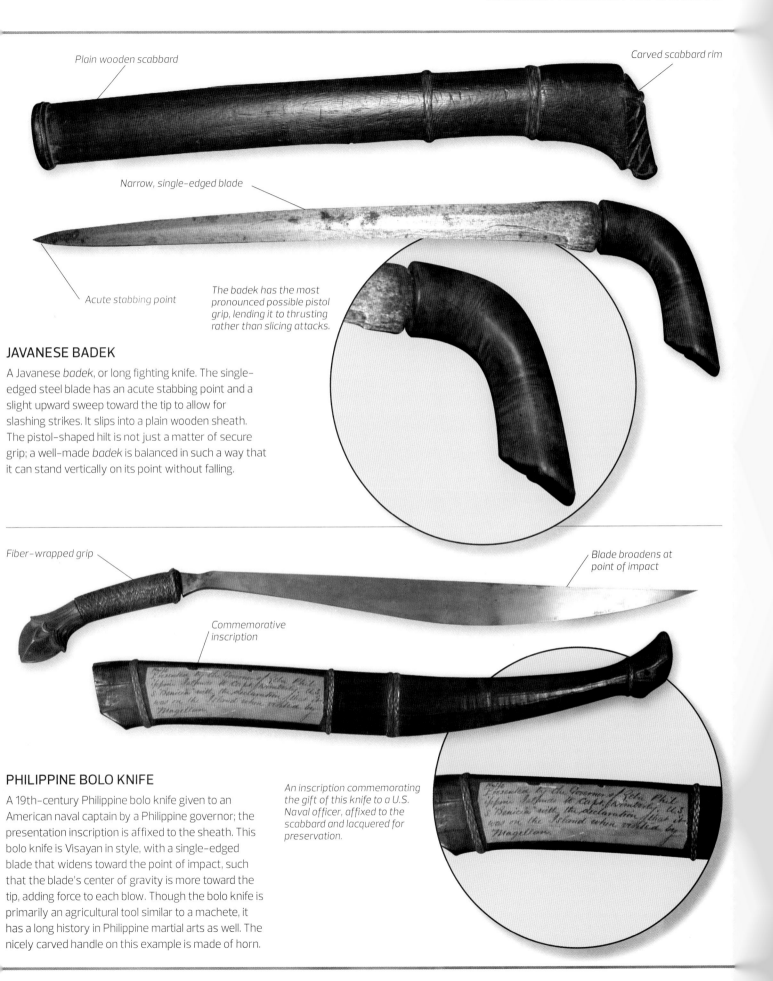

Plain wooden scabbard

Carved scabbard rim

Narrow, single-edged blade

Acute stabbing point

The badek has the most pronounced possible pistol grip, lending it to thrusting rather than slicing attacks.

JAVANESE BADEK

A Javanese *badek*, or long fighting knife. The single-edged steel blade has an acute stabbing point and a slight upward sweep toward the tip to allow for slashing strikes. It slips into a plain wooden sheath. The pistol-shaped hilt is not just a matter of secure grip; a well-made *badek* is balanced in such a way that it can stand vertically on its point without falling.

Fiber-wrapped grip

Blade broadens at point of impact

Commemorative inscription

PHILIPPINE BOLO KNIFE

A 19th-century Philippine bolo knife given to an American naval captain by a Philippine governor; the presentation inscription is affixed to the sheath. This bolo knife is Visayan in style, with a single-edged blade that widens toward the point of impact, such that the blade's center of gravity is more toward the tip, adding force to each blow. Though the bolo knife is primarily an agricultural tool similar to a machete, it has a long history in Philippine martial arts as well. The nicely carved handle on this example is made of horn.

An inscription commemorating the gift of this knife to a U.S. Naval officer, affixed to the scabbard and lacquered for preservation.

The Kriss

n Indonesia and neighboring countries, the *kriss*, or *keris*, is a weapon with a long history and extraordinary symbolic value. Simultaneously an effective weapon, an art object, and a spiritual artifact, the *kriss* is regarded with the same reverence in some Southeast Asian cultures that the samurai sword commands in Japanese traditions. *Kriss* blades are forged by master smiths of iron and nickel, usually in numerous folded layers. While the archaeological record indicates that early blades were usually straight, the typical *kriss* has a wavy blade in a style reminiscent of the flame blades of Europe. A wavy *kriss* blade must have an odd number of curves, which are intended to inflict maximum damage in a strike but also to invoke the *nāga*, or dragon spirit. In this way, the *kriss* is regarded as a spiritually charged entity. But these knives are also prized possessions in a material sense; a fine blade mounted in precious metals and exotic hardwoods is a badge of wealth and rank.

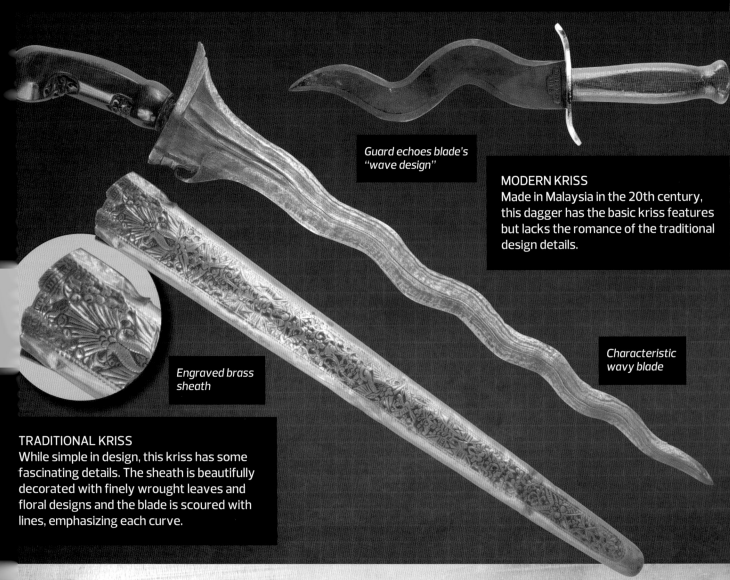

Guard echoes blade's "wave design"

MODERN KRISS
Made in Malaysia in the 20th century, this dagger has the basic kriss features but lacks the romance of the traditional design details.

Engraved brass sheath

Characteristic wavy blade

TRADITIONAL KRISS
While simple in design, this kriss has some fascinating details. The sheath is beautifully decorated with finely wrought leaves and floral designs and the blade is scoured with lines, emphasizing each curve.

DEMON HILT
A Balinese or Malay kriss. The hilt is carved in the form of a demon and inlaid with semiprecious stones.

Demonic figure holds wooden sheath

15-inch blade

The sheath is adorned with jet and topped with polished wood.

Simple wooden hilt

ELEGANT KRISS
The design of the traditional kriss spread to neighboring regions of Southeast Asia, such as the Philippines. Intended for stabbing, the blade is of variable length. In a curved–blade kriss, each bend is called a *luk*. This is a comparatively simple design with restrained carving on the hilt and a straight brass sheath.

KRISS STAND
A Balinese kriss in its stand, which is carved in the figure of a dancer. In Malay and other cultures, the kriss was considered to be a living thing, with the power to bring good or bad luck, or even to operate on its own.

The sheath is topped with an attractively grained, curved block of wood, known in Malay as a wranga. The wranga is said to symbolize a boat, representing the seafaring history of the Malay people.

Daggers of the Americas

North and South America are home to a dazzling variety of cultures and traditions. From the ritual blades of the Incas and Aztecs to the knives of the North American tribes, they show a range of styles from the most strikingly cultic to the utilitarian, and often display the sort of cultural cross-pollination that characterizes much of the cultural heritage of these two continents.

The skill of the Chimu artisans is evident in the elegant gold openwork of the hilt, with both organic and rectilinear designs.

Gold hilt in the figure of priest or deity

The unusual pommel carved to resemble a human head suggests European influence on the knifemaker.

Beaded sash featuring classic geometric decorative motifs

Soft, beaded sheath

GOLD TUMI OF THE CHIMU

A gold *tumi*, or sacrificial knife, of the Chimu people, closely related to the Inca. Tumi knives were used by Precolumbian civilizations of the Andes for annual rituals in which black or white llamas were sacrificed to ensure fertility in the coming year. Many tumi were made of precious materials and included in burials of prominent people; this typical example has a handle in the form of a priest figure, inlayed with turquoise. The tumi has since become a national symbol of Peru.

Gold blade is purely ceremonial

GREAT LAKES KNIFE IN WAMPUM SHEATH

An 18th-century Native American dagger from what is now the Canadian portion of the Great Lakes region. The blade's wooden hilt has a faceted grip and a pommel carved in the shape of a human head. Of particular interest are the sheath and the baldric from which it is suspended; both are made of animal hide, adorned with porcupine quills and patterns of decorative beads. Overall, this is an excellent example of regional Native American decorative art.

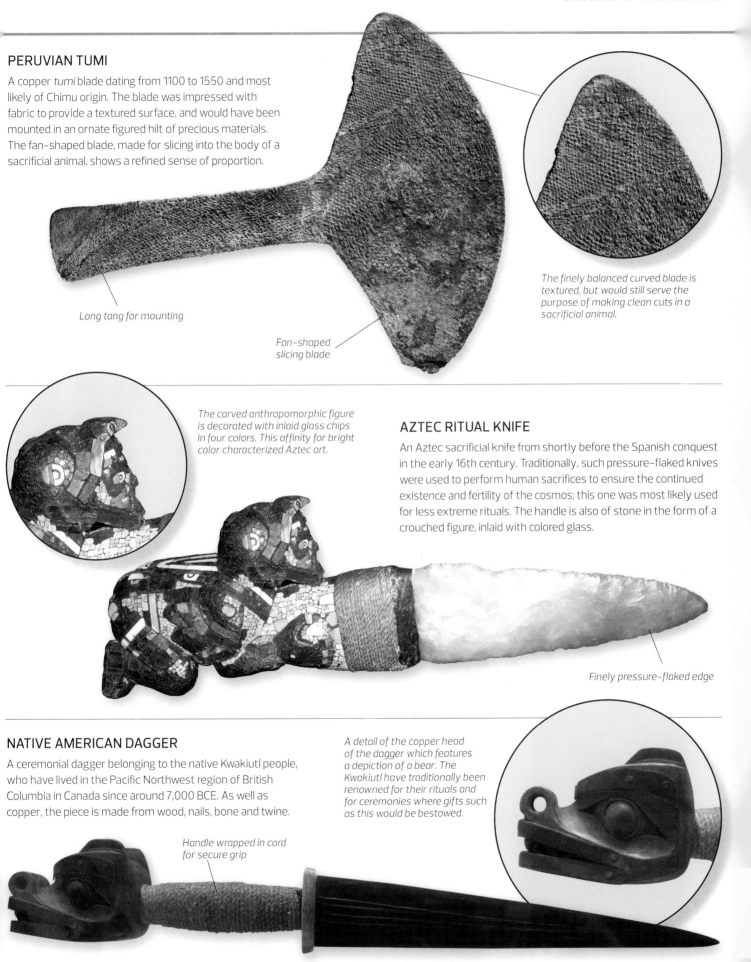

PERUVIAN TUMI

A copper *tumi* blade dating from 1100 to 1550 and most likely of Chimu origin. The blade was impressed with fabric to provide a textured surface, and would have been mounted in an ornate figured hilt of precious materials. The fan-shaped blade, made for slicing into the body of a sacrificial animal, shows a refined sense of proportion.

The finely balanced curved blade is textured, but would still serve the purpose of making clean cuts in a sacrificial animal.

Long tang for mounting

Fan-shaped slicing blade

The carved anthropomorphic figure is decorated with inlaid glass chips in four colors. This affinity for bright color characterized Aztec art.

AZTEC RITUAL KNIFE

An Aztec sacrificial knife from shortly before the Spanish conquest in the early 16th century. Traditionally, such pressure-flaked knives were used to perform human sacrifices to ensure the continued existence and fertility of the cosmos; this one was most likely used for less extreme rituals. The handle is also of stone in the form of a crouched figure, inlaid with colored glass.

Finely pressure-flaked edge

NATIVE AMERICAN DAGGER

A ceremonial dagger belonging to the native Kwakiutl people, who have lived in the Pacific Northwest region of British Columbia in Canada since around 7,000 BCE. As well as copper, the piece is made from wood, nails, bone and twine.

A detail of the copper head of the dagger which features a depiction of a bear. The Kwakiutl have traditionally been renowned for their rituals and for ceremonies where gifts such as this would be bestowed.

Handle wrapped in cord for secure grip

Clubs from Around the World

The axe and club are near-universal weapons, and they have taken a vast number of forms in cultures around the world. In North America, the tomahawk and the war club were the centerpieces of much inter-tribal conflict; in the Pacific, the war club is the archetypal weapon. All of these weapons recall martial traditions in which close combat, involving a life-or-death contest between two warriors at a time, was the measure of a warrior's prowess.

The club's hitting surface is the animal's snout

AFRICAN CLUB

This distinctive club is a simple representation of the head of a cow or bull. As symbols of a person's wealth, cattle have always been very important to African tribespeople so it is likely that this club belonged to an important member of the tribe and would have been used for ceremonial purposes. It was made in the 19th century.

IRON AFRICAN CLUB

Made in the early 19th century, this iron club is the work of a skilled artisan. Along with snakes on the handle, its head has an intricate plaited ribbon ornamentation.

The butt end of the shaft is cast with a small decorative knob

Snakes ascend the handle

MAORI PATU

he short-handled war club, or *patu*, was the principal weapon of the Maori people of New Zealand. It could be carved from the wood of the kauri tree, jade, or whalebone as in the example shown here. The hole in the handle would have accommodated a leather thong attaching the weapon to the warrior's wrist.

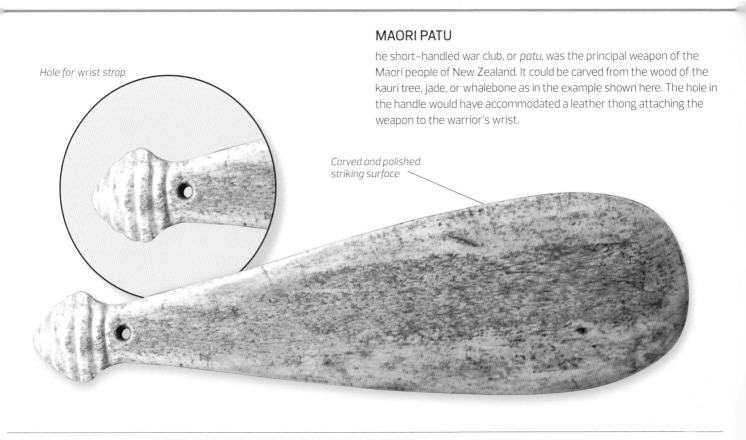

Hole for wrist strap

Carved and polished striking surface

TONGAN PAKIPAKI

This *pakipaki* is a fine example of a paddle club. The rounded upper end of this pakipaki is distinguished by finely carved decoration over its entire surface, and has a transverse ridged collar or cross rib. Polynesian warriors used a wide variety of clubs and sometimes decorated them with teeth taken from slain enemies.

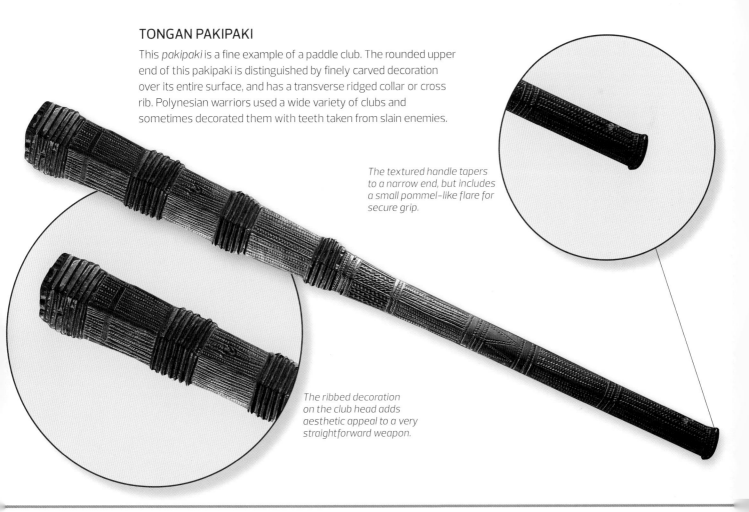

The textured handle tapers to a narrow end, but includes a small pommel-like flare for secure grip.

The ribbed decoration on the club head adds aesthetic appeal to a very straightforward weapon.

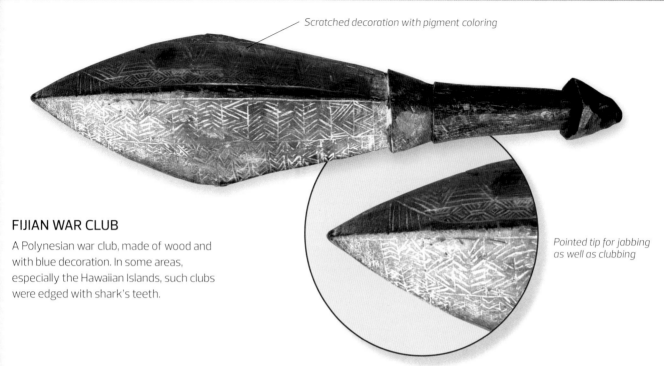

Scratched decoration with pigment coloring

FIJIAN WAR CLUB

A Polynesian war club, made of wood and with blue decoration. In some areas, especially the Hawaiian Islands, such clubs were edged with shark's teeth.

Pointed tip for jabbing as well as clubbing

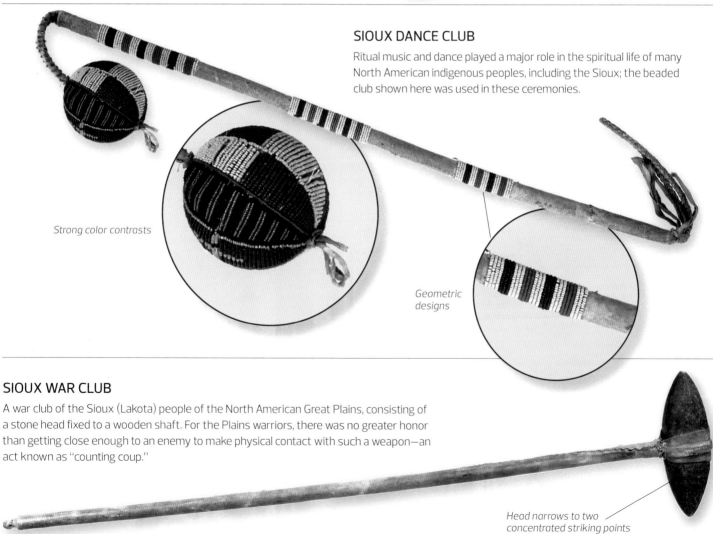

SIOUX DANCE CLUB

Ritual music and dance played a major role in the spiritual life of many North American indigenous peoples, including the Sioux; the beaded club shown here was used in these ceremonies.

Strong color contrasts

Geometric designs

SIOUX WAR CLUB

A war club of the Sioux (Lakota) people of the North American Great Plains, consisting of a stone head fixed to a wooden shaft. For the Plains warriors, there was no greater honor than getting close enough to an enemy to make physical contact with such a weapon—an act known as "counting coup."

Head narrows to two concentrated striking points

TLINGIT CLUB

A ceremonial war club of the Tlingit people of southern Alaska. Tlingit clubs were made of a variety of materials, including ivory and bone, and a special type of club was used in rituals to kill enemy captives taken in battle.

A leather wrist strap helped keep the club securely in its wielder's control.

Simple linear artwork

CEREMONIAL CLUB

The war club was a common weapon among many North American peoples; shown here is a distinct example from the Pacific Northwest. The carving and decoration indicate it might have been for ceremonial use.

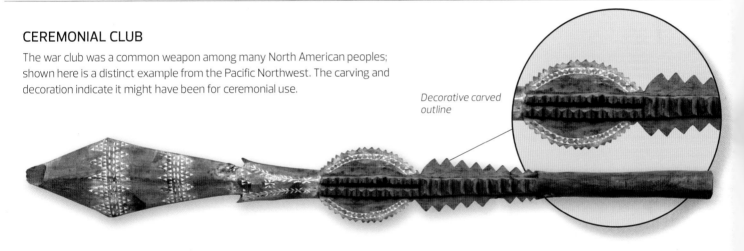

Decorative carved outline

INDIAN WOODEN CLUB

This wooden club from India has been carefully carved with plenty of decorative detailing around the head and on the handle. Viewed from the top the head resembles a sunflower. This amount of ornamentation suggests that the club had a use beyond mere protection and warfare. It dates from the late 19th century.

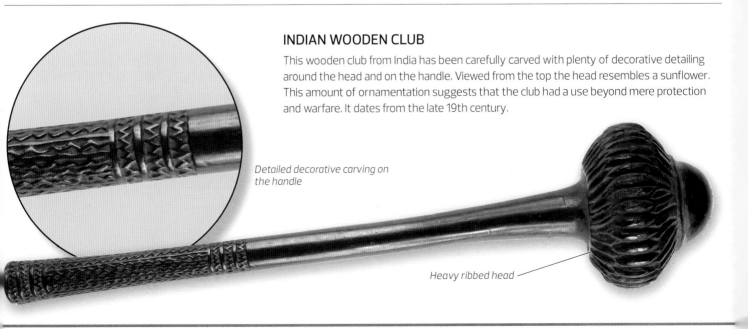

Detailed decorative carving on the handle

Heavy ribbed head

The Modern Dagger

Knives for a New Age

The modern era has seen bladed weapons largely eclipsed by firearms; as a result, daggers have been largely divided between functional combat and survival knives and expensive, often artisan-made art knives. The former category includes such famed combat knives as the Fairbairn-Sykes and the K-Bar, as well as the bayonet.

The latter class includes daggers made of expensive and exotic materials, sometimes designed or crafted by renowned artists, and intended solely as objects of beauty. Another kind of dagger—the highly specialized and often ingenious weapons designed for specific purposes, including those of espionage—has developed in fascinating ways over the course of the past century.

THE SECOND OF MAY 1808, or *The Charge of the Mamelukes* by Francisco Goya. Painted in 1814, it commemorates an uprising of Spanish citizens against Napoleon's forces that had just taken control of the Spanish throne. In the painting, both Spanish citizens and French Mamelukes—depicted here as Moorish—use daggers in the vicious melee.

18th-Century European Daggers

In the 17th and 18th centuries, the small sword became the dominant hilt weapon, superseding the rapier and making the dagger a far less prominent component of the European fencing traditions. The trend was only exacerbated by the increasing efficiency and compactness of firearms, which became the preferred weapons for dueling. While daggers continued to be issued in certain militaries, especially navies, civilian daggers were increasingly employed either as concealed weapons or as art objects.

RUSSIAN STILETTO

In 1712, Tsar Peter the Great visited the city of Tula in western Russia and ordered that the area's blacksmiths establish the first modern armaments factory in Russia. Tula rapidly established itself as the foremost metalworking center in the nation, producing not only arms but also household items such as tea urns. This stiletto is a distinctly Russian weapon from those production facilities. The hollow-ground, triangular blade, similar to that of a small sword, is made purely for stabbing rather than slicing. The mountings are of gold vermeil—sterling silver plated with gold—with a grip of hand-painted porcelain.

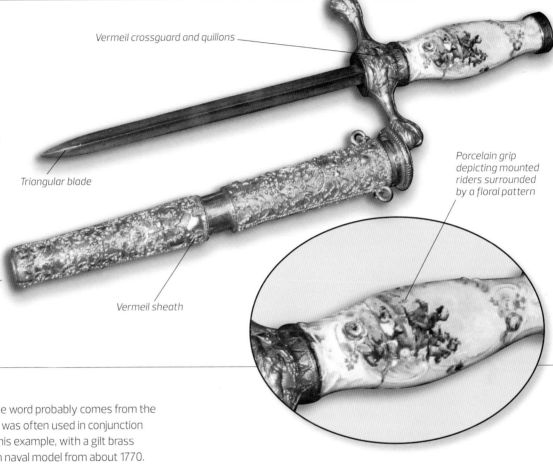

Vermeil crossguard and quillons

Triangular blade

Vermeil sheath

Porcelain grip depicting mounted riders surrounded by a floral pattern

BRITISH NAVAL DIRK

A relatively long knife, the dirk (the word probably comes from the Gaelic *sgian dearg*, or "red knife") was often used in conjunction with the claymore broadsword. This example, with a gilt brass handle with ivory grips, is a British naval model from about 1770.

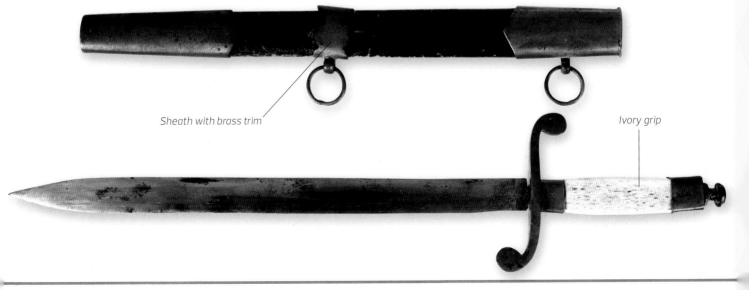

Sheath with brass trim

Ivory grip

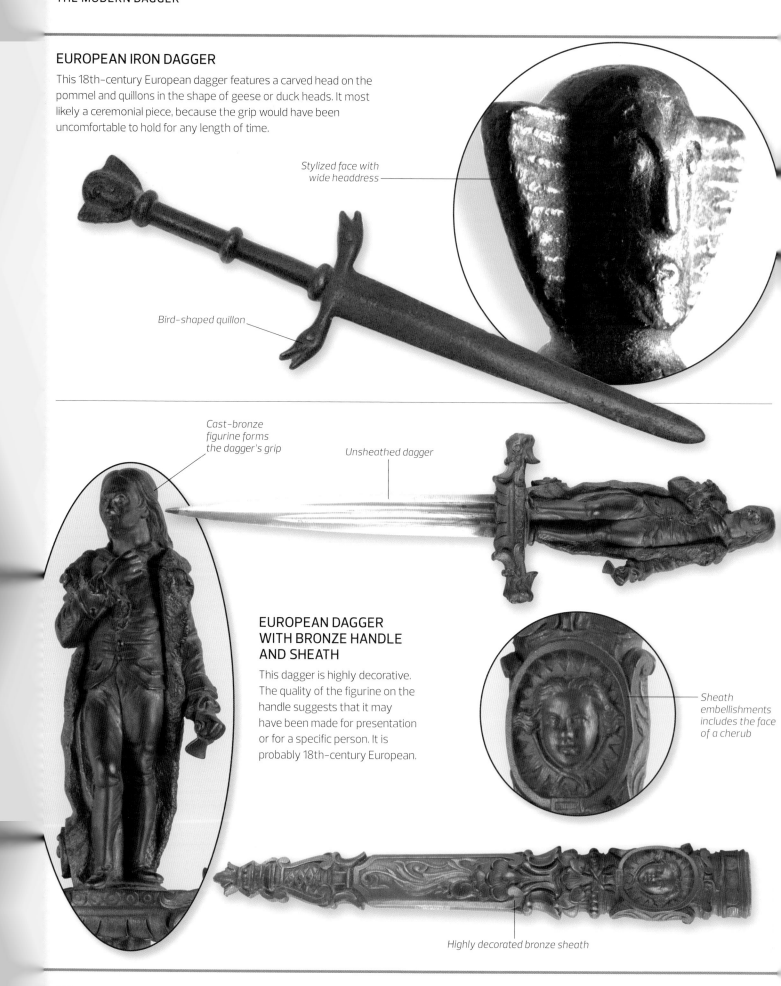

EUROPEAN IRON DAGGER

This 18th-century European dagger features a carved head on the pommel and quillons in the shape of geese or duck heads. It most likely a ceremonial piece, because the grip would have been uncomfortable to hold for any length of time.

Stylized face with wide headdress

Bird-shaped quillon

Cast-bronze figurine forms the dagger's grip

Unsheathed dagger

EUROPEAN DAGGER WITH BRONZE HANDLE AND SHEATH

This dagger is highly decorative. The quality of the figurine on the handle suggests that it may have been made for presentation or for a specific person. It is probably 18th-century European.

Sheath embellishments includes the face of a cherub

Highly decorated bronze sheath

19th-Century European Daggers

In the 19th century, the dagger became, more than ever, an art object. Of little practical use except as a concealed weapon, it nonetheless took creative impetus from the Romantic fascination with medieval culture, Orientalist exoticism and even the aesthetic "decadence" of the later part of the century. The results were various and fascinating: recreations of Renaissance stilettos existed alongside wildly impractical and ornate blades and expensive, beautifully fashioned mountings that were of more interest than the blades they contained.

ORNATE DANISH DAGGER HILT

A magnificent dagger hilt made in Copenhagen by Magnus Hansen in the late 1800s. The hilt is of walrus ivory, intricately carved into a full-length image of the Norwegian naval hero Peter Wessel Tordenskjold (1690–1720), who achieved fame for his daring exploits in the Great Northern War before being killed in a duel at the age of 30. The scrolled crossguard is of gold vermeil, and the hollow-ground triangular blade fits into a sheath of carved walrus ivory.

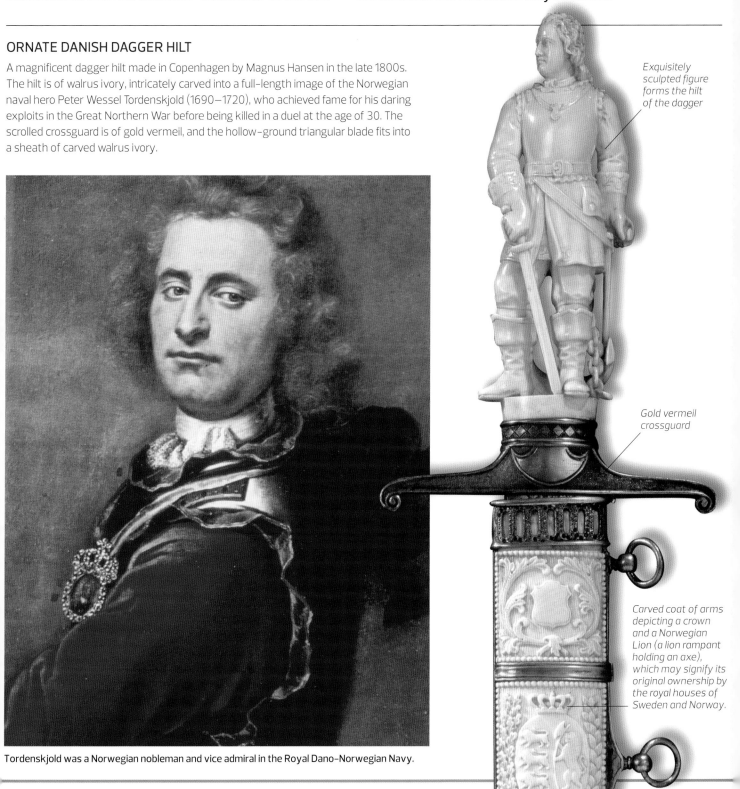

Exquisitely sculpted figure forms the hilt of the dagger

Gold vermeil crossguard

Carved coat of arms depicting a crown and a Norwegian Lion (a lion rampant holding an axe), which may signify its original ownership by the royal houses of Sweden and Norway.

Tordenskjold was a Norwegian nobleman and vice admiral in the Royal Dano-Norwegian Navy.

SPANISH FIGHTING KNIVES

This pair of 19th-century Spanish fighting knives feature pointed gazelle horn handles that are both decorative and practical. The natural striations allow a firm grip, and their tips can puncture almost as well as the blades.

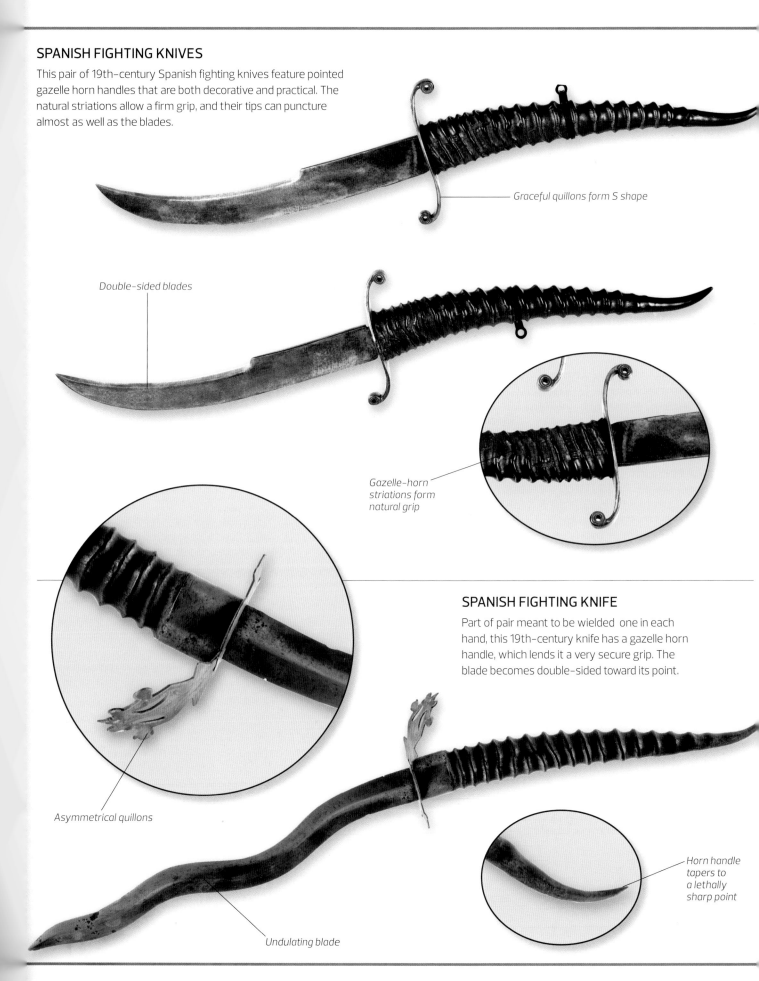

Graceful quillons form S shape

Double-sided blades

Gazelle-horn striations form natural grip

Asymmetrical quillons

SPANISH FIGHTING KNIFE

Part of pair meant to be wielded one in each hand, this 19th-century knife has a gazelle horn handle, which lends it a very secure grip. The blade becomes double-sided toward its point.

Horn handle tapers to a lethally sharp point

Undulating blade

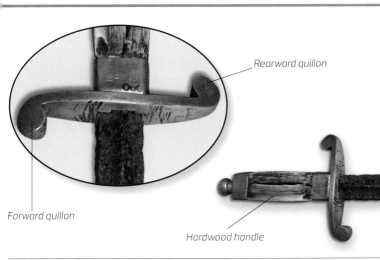

Rearward quillon

Forward quillon

Hardwood handle

Triangular blade

RUSSIAN NAVAL DIRK

A 19th-century Russian naval officer's dirk in a style characteristic of such weapons throughout Europe. The hollow-ground triangular blade is fitted to a brass guard with one forward and one rearward quillon, a hardwood handle and a brass button pommel. This sturdy weapon was invaluable in 19th-century naval warfare, which still occasionally involved hand-to-hand combat during the boarding of hostile ships.

COSSACK KINDJAL

Sometimes called the "Circassian dagger," from its origin with the Circassian people of the Caucasus Mountains, the kindjal was adopted by the Cossacks of the Russian Empire from the 18th century onward. This 19th-century example has a 14-inch blade and a hilt inlaid with semiprecious stones. In the hands of Cossack warriors, it was used in conjunction with the shashka sword.

Gem-studded hilt

Fuller

RUSSIAN ROMAN-STYLE DAGGER

Created in the era of the Russian-Caucasian wars (1816–1864) this beautiful 19th-century dagger is made of Damascus steel in the form of a Roman sword. The grip is made of silver, and the sheath is also decorated with silver.

Blade of Damascus steel

Sheath

Silver handle

Medallion decoration on hilt

Rudimentary etching on crossguard

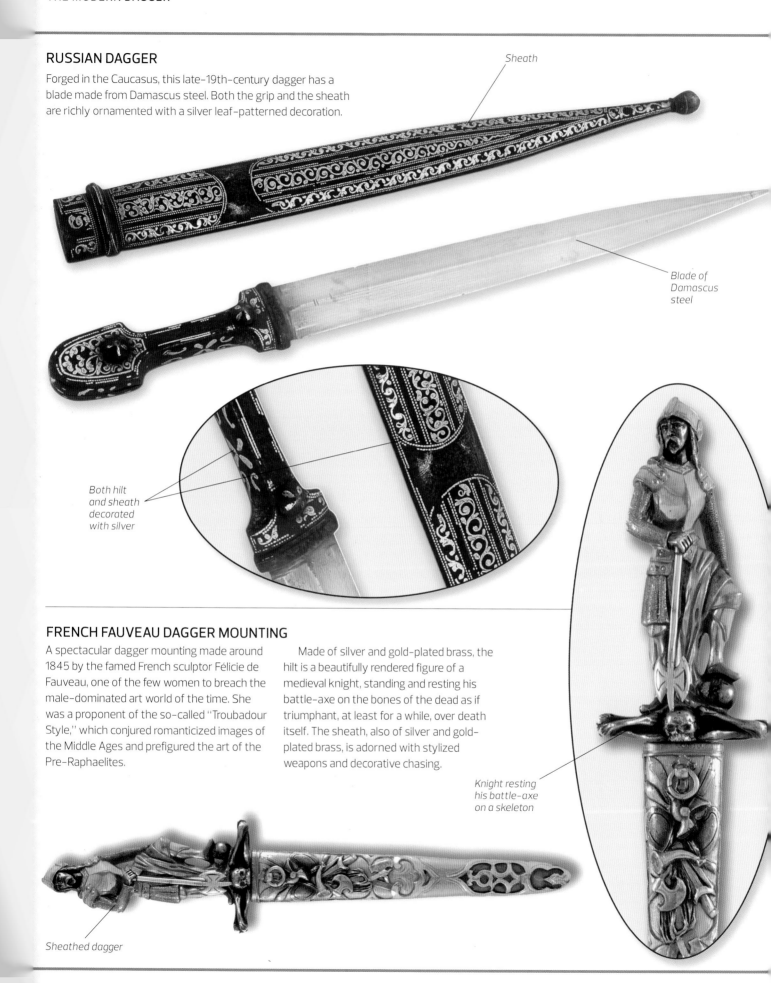

RUSSIAN DAGGER

Forged in the Caucasus, this late–19th–century dagger has a blade made from Damascus steel. Both the grip and the sheath are richly ornamented with a silver leaf–patterned decoration.

Sheath

Blade of Damascus steel

Both hilt and sheath decorated with silver

FRENCH FAUVEAU DAGGER MOUNTING

A spectacular dagger mounting made around 1845 by the famed French sculptor Félicie de Fauveau, one of the few women to breach the male-dominated art world of the time. She was a proponent of the so-called "Troubadour Style," which conjured romanticized images of the Middle Ages and prefigured the art of the Pre-Raphaelites.

Made of silver and gold-plated brass, the hilt is a beautifully rendered figure of a medieval knight, standing and resting his battle-axe on the bones of the dead as if triumphant, at least for a while, over death itself. The sheath, also of silver and gold-plated brass, is adorned with stylized weapons and decorative chasing.

Knight resting his battle-axe on a skeleton

Sheathed dagger

BRITISH FLICK-DAGGER

This combination weapon has a malacca cane shaft, with weighted ends decorated with a decorative cord binding. The dagger is retained by a spring catch and released with a flick of the wrist. It was made in Britain around 1850.

Woven rattan

Malacca cane shaft

Spring-released dagger

SCOTTISH DIRK

The Scottish dirk is the traditional and ceremonial dress dagger of the officers of Scottish Highland regiments. The shape of the grip forms the shape of a thistle, the national emblem of Scotland. Ornate fittings, such as the silver embellishments on this 19th-century example, became popular shortly after 1800. Along with the dirk, the sheath has added compartments to hold a matching small knife and a two-pronged fork.

Thistle-patterned pommel

Sheathed dirk

Sheath with compartments for dagger, small knife and fork

Fork

Small knife

Colonel Alexander Ranaldson MacDonell of Glengarry (1773–1828), clan chief of Clan MacDonell of Glengarry, wearing Highland dress, including a dirk with three compartments at his waist

Sheathed dirk

The Bayonet

At the First Battle of Manassas (Bull Run), Confederate General Thomas J. "Stonewall" Jackson was told by a panicked fellow officer that Union troops were advancing very close to Confederate lines. Jackson replied with characteristic cool, "Then, Sir, we shall give them the bayonet." It was a chilling line, for the bayonet, introduced to the battlefield in the 17th century when reloading a musket took considerable time, was regarded as a barbaric weapon in the 19th century, to be employed only in dire necessity. Already, a variety of blade lengths and mounting techniques had been developed, however, and in well-trained hands a bayonet could be remarkably effective in close combat. Bayonet charges had become a standard military tactic in the 18th century, and would occasionally figure in the Civil War and beyond; they have even been used effectively by British troops in the 21st century war in Afghanistan. As savage as they seem, bayonets are merely a return to the spears and pikes of earlier martial traditions. When detached from the gun, many bayonets are designed to double as a utility knife or dagger.

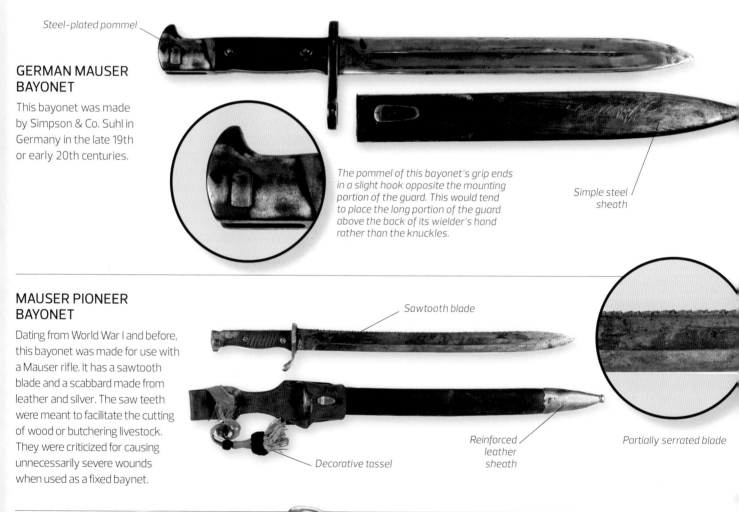

Steel-plated pommel

GERMAN MAUSER BAYONET

This bayonet was made by Simpson & Co. Suhl in Germany in the late 19th or early 20th centuries.

The pommel of this bayonet's grip ends in a slight hook opposite the mounting portion of the guard. This would tend to place the long portion of the guard above the back of its wielder's hand rather than the knuckles.

Simple steel sheath

MAUSER PIONEER BAYONET

Dating from World War I and before, this bayonet was made for use with a Mauser rifle. It has a sawtooth blade and a scabbard made from leather and silver. The saw teeth were meant to facilitate the cutting of wood or butchering livestock. They were criticized for causing unnecessarily severe wounds when used as a fixed baynet.

Sawtooth blade

Decorative tassel

Reinforced leather sheath

Partially serrated blade

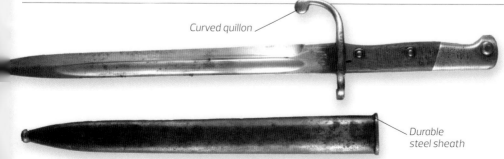

Curved quillon

Durable steel sheath

KNIFE BAYONET AND SHEATH

Weyersberg, Kirschbaum & Co. (WKC) began making swords in Solingen, Germany, over two hundred years ago. They made this bayonet in the late 19th century, and it went on to be used during World War I.

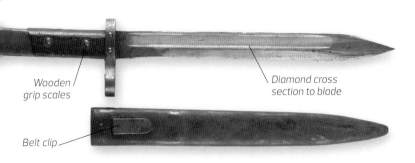

Wooden grip scales

Diamond cross section to blade

Belt clip

STEYR–MANNLICHER BAYONET

This wooden-handled bayonet was made for the Steyr-Mannlicher M1895 bolt-action rifle. It is marked "FG GY" indicating it was made in Hungary; bayonets for this rifle were also made in Austria.

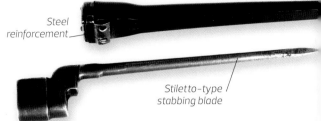

Steel reinforcement

Stiletto-type stabbing blade

WW2 MKII SPIKE BAYONET

This spike-type bayonet, in which the bayonet and socket were one solid forging, was made for use with the Short Magazine Lee-Enfield rifle (SMLE) Mark IV, during World War II. Over three million were made. The sheath is not the standard version and was probably manufactured separately.

Tough leather sheath

Triangular blade

A close view of the flat spring clip for fixing the bayonet. Should the bayonet be used as a hand weapon, this metal tang and clip would serve as the grip.

WW2 JOHNSON BAYONET

Military Issue M1941 Johnson Rifle bayonet from the U.S. is produced from a single billet of steel that is forged into shape. It has no defined handle or grip, just a flat extension. This was clearly not intended as an all-round utility weapon.

The stylized eagle head sculpted on the hilt was a symbol of the Weimar Republic between the wars.

WEIMAR POLICE BAYONET

The hilt of this German Police bayonet is in the form of an Eagle, symbol of the Weimar Republic, Germany's government from the end of World War I until the establishment of the Third Reich in 1933.

Long, triangular blade

Strong protective sheath

Brass grip

LEBEL BAYONETS

These bayonets were produced in 1916 for use with the 8mm French Lebel Model 1886 bolt-action rifle. The metal grip was produced in both nickel and brass, as supplies of the metals dictated.

American Daggers

The modern American dagger is a mythologized weapon. Whether in the hands of Civil War soldiers, frontiersmen, or South American gauchos, it represents not only rugged individualism but also an untamed, primal engagement with nature and one's enemies. In North, Central, and South America, daggers were often rather crudely made in home workshops, but they were also mass-produced and distributed across the continent and even overseas.

Crude clip-point blade

Simple, functional sheath

19TH-CENTURY CONFEDERATE KNIVES

Confederate privates carried these crude knives, which may well have been made from a saw or farm-implement blade. The design of many Southern knives was inspired by the famous Bowie knife, the long-bladed weapon popularized by the frontiersmen Jim and Rezin Bowie in the 1830s.

Crude clip-point blade

Wire wrap on handle

Bone scales on handle

Brass guard

Wide groove in blade

Hand-stitched leather sheath

CONFEDERATE KNIVES

Two knives from the Civil War. The simpler weapon (above) is a crudely fashioned Bowie knife, with a clip-point blade and a handle made of two bone scales riveted to the tang. The other weapon is a stout officer's dagger from the Confederate navy. Its clip-point blade, reminiscent of a Bowie knife, is altogether more precisely made, with a wide central groove, a slightly upturned tip, and a sturdy bolster. It is fitted with a sabre-style grip and round guard.

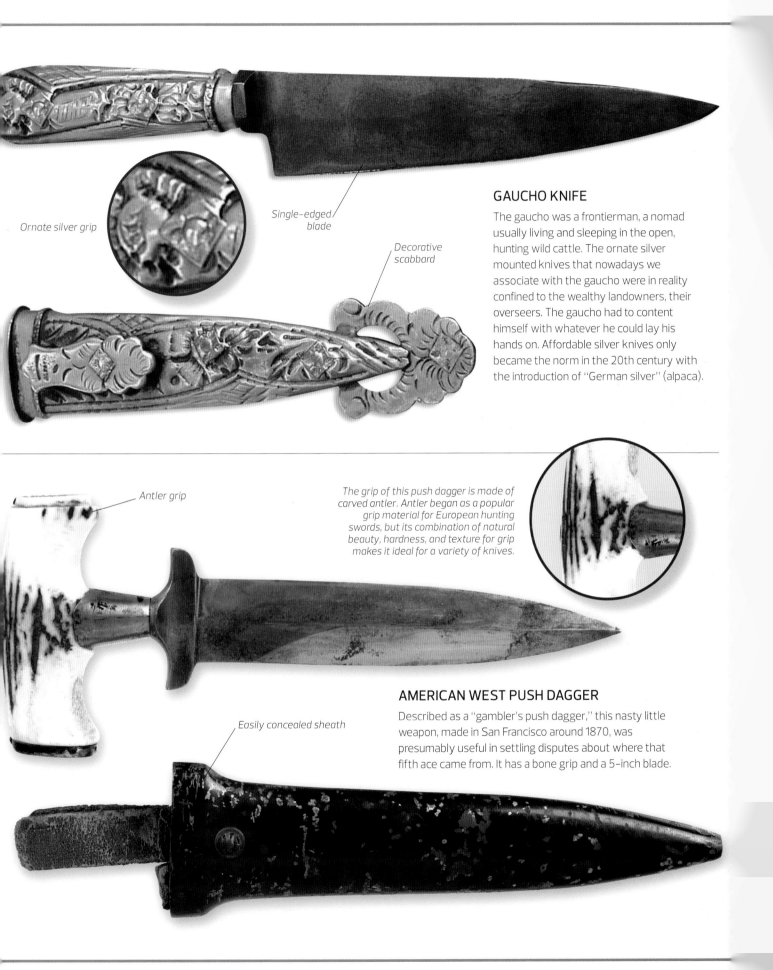

Ornate silver grip

Single-edged blade

Decorative scabbard

GAUCHO KNIFE

The gaucho was a frontierman, a nomad usually living and sleeping in the open, hunting wild cattle. The ornate silver mounted knives that nowadays we associate with the gaucho were in reality confined to the wealthy landowners, their overseers. The gaucho had to content himself with whatever he could lay his hands on. Affordable silver knives only became the norm in the 20th century with the introduction of "German silver" (alpaca).

Antler grip

The grip of this push dagger is made of carved antler. Antler began as a popular grip material for European hunting swords, but its combination of natural beauty, hardness, and texture for grip makes it ideal for a variety of knives.

AMERICAN WEST PUSH DAGGER

Described as a "gambler's push dagger," this nasty little weapon, made in San Francisco around 1870, was presumably useful in settling disputes about where that fifth ace came from. It has a bone grip and a 5-inch blade.

Easily concealed sheath

The Bowie Knife

No American knife is more iconic than the Bowie knife. Though invented by Rezin Bowie, it was most famously associated with his brother, the frontiersman and fighter Jim Bowie, who died fighting in the Alamo in 1836. In 1827, Jim wielded a large Bowie knife in the Sandbar Fight, a brief melee that erupted in the aftermath of a bloodless duel for which Bowie had served as a second; though both shot and stabbed, Bowie killed one man, injured another, and survived. The basic form of the Bowie knife—a sheath knife with a clip-point blade and simple crossguard—has endured ever since, though modern versions are considerably smaller than those favored in the 19th-century American west.

Wide, sturdy spine to blade

Drop-point blade tip

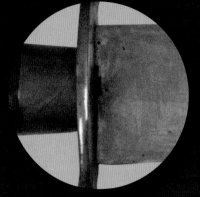

The hilt juncture reveals how slender the blade's tang is

Highly acute clip-point blade

19TH-CENTURY BOWIE KNIFE : The Bowie knife is named for James Bowie who was killed during the Siege of Fort Alamo in Texas in 1836. It is a hunting knife with a long blade, short hilt, and a grip usually with wooden or horn sidepieces. The design is popular and frequently copied, as in the case of this late 19th century version from eastern Europe.

Elegant hardwood handle

CONTEMPORARY BOWIE : An elegant contemporary Bowie knife made by Carter Cutlery. The blade is pattern-welded (a type often mistakenly called Damascus), and ends in a drop point rather than the more common clip point. The hilt is luxurious if understated, with a brass guard and a handle made of three different kinds of exotic hardwood. A gently rounded brass pommel adds balance to both hand and eye.

WILD BILL AND HIS BOWIE KNIFE : Wild Bill Hickock (1837–1876) was a famed gambler, gunslinger, and lawman of the Old West. Though many of his exploits were fictional, he possessed—and profited from—considerable skills in all those areas until his murder by a fellow gambler. In this portrait, he wears two revolvers slung handle-forward and a large Bowie knife. The knife is most likely worn for effect—no such blade would be tucked into a belt unsheathed—but it indicates how fearsome a large Bowie knife would appear on the belt or in the hand of an opponent.

Manufacturer's mark at base of blade

Stacked leather grip

Mark indicating the blade's origin

Curved, acute blade tip

CONTEMPORARY SOG BOWIE : A contemporary Bowie knife manufactured by the well-regarded firm SOG. The knife is significantly smaller in scale than most 19th-century versions; its clip-point blade, made of stainless steel in Seki, Japan, is fitted to a strong hilt with an understated crossguard and a stacked leather grip. A wrist thong can be secured to the pommel.

Brass shoe on sheath

REZIN BOWIE

Rezin Bowie (1793–1841), brother of Jim Bowie and inventor of the Bowie knife. Though he never became as famous as his brother, who died in the Alamo, Rezin was the originator of this iconic American blade. The exact design of the earliest weapons is still subject to speculation, but it could not have been much different from the clip-point blades that became synonymous with the Bowie knife.

20th-Century Fighting Knives

The 20th century may have seen an unparalleled increase in the technological sophistication and large-scale destruction of war, but the reality of combat still involved hand-to-hand fighting, and combat knives took a variety of forms. Some, such as the fabled Sykes-Fairbairn, were sleek and elegant, with spear-point blades; others doubled as survival knives, and often had clip-point or drop-point blades that made them useful for a range of tasks. The type of knife varied according to the specialization of its owner and the demands of the operational theater. Design features sometimes included such details as knuckle guards that could be used as striking surfaces, and hollow handles that contained small survival tools. Some knives doubled as presentation weapons, becoming badges of membership in an elite fighting force.

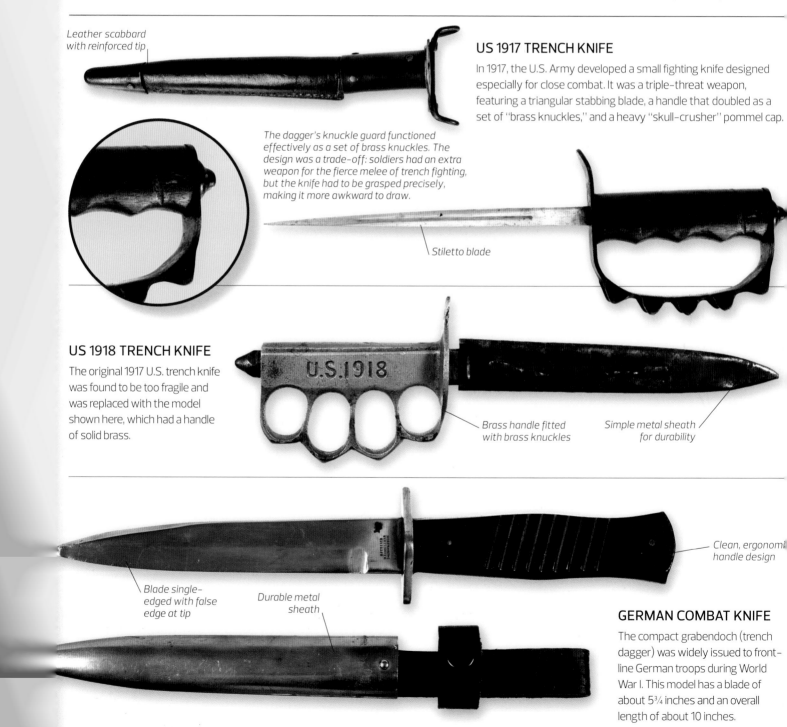

Leather scabbard with reinforced tip

US 1917 TRENCH KNIFE

In 1917, the U.S. Army developed a small fighting knife designed especially for close combat. It was a triple-threat weapon, featuring a triangular stabbing blade, a handle that doubled as a set of "brass knuckles," and a heavy "skull-crusher" pommel cap.

The dagger's knuckle guard functioned effectively as a set of brass knuckles. The design was a trade-off: soldiers had an extra weapon for the fierce melee of trench fighting, but the knife had to be grasped precisely, making it more awkward to draw.

Stiletto blade

US 1918 TRENCH KNIFE

The original 1917 U.S. trench knife was found to be too fragile and was replaced with the model shown here, which had a handle of solid brass.

Brass handle fitted with brass knuckles

Simple metal sheath for durability

Blade single-edged with false edge at tip

Durable metal sheath

Clean, ergonomic handle design

GERMAN COMBAT KNIFE

The compact grabendoch (trench dagger) was widely issued to front-line German troops during World War I. This model has a blade of about 5¾ inches and an overall length of about 10 inches.

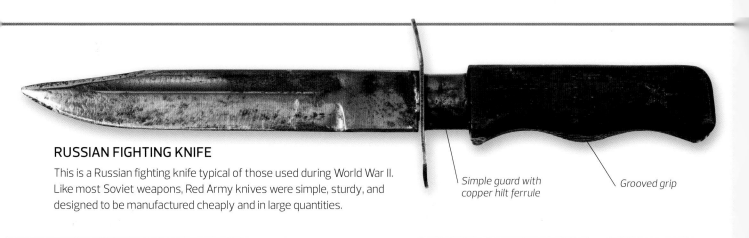

RUSSIAN FIGHTING KNIFE

This is a Russian fighting knife typical of those used during World War II. Like most Soviet weapons, Red Army knives were simple, sturdy, and designed to be manufactured cheaply and in large quantities.

Simple guard with copper hilt ferrule

Grooved grip

Etched insignia on blade

Distinctive flanged grip

Narrow, spear-point blade

This knife is adorned with the badge of the Special Air Service (SAS), the elite commando force of the British military. The SAS motto, "Who dares wins," has become the motto of several related special forces around the world.

SYKES-FAIRBAIRN

One of the most famous knives of World War II, the Sykes-Fairbairn Commando Knife was widely used by U.S. and British special forces. Developed by two experts in hand-to-hand combat (see below) it was a lightweight, stainless-steel weapon. The slender 7½-inch blade was designed especially to slip between the ribs of an opponent.

W. E. FAIRBAIRN AND ERIC SYKES

While serving as a police officer in Shanghai, China, in the early 1900s, William Ewart Fairbairn became one of the first Westerners to achieve proficiency in Asian martial arts. (Ironically, in light of later events, he initially trained with a Japanese instructor.) Fairbairn eventually rose to command the Shanghai Municipal Police, and together with his colleague Eric Sykes, began training his officers in hybrid hand-to-hand fighting techniques they named the "Defendu System." With the coming of World War II, Sykes and Fairbairn were recalled to Britain, where they began teaching their system to the newly formed Commandos. During this time, the duo designed the famous dagger-style knife that bears their names. With the U.S. entry into the war, Fairbairn left for America to train the OSS (Office of Strategic Services); Sykes stayed on to work with SOE (Special Operations Executive) and SIS (Secret Intelligence Service).

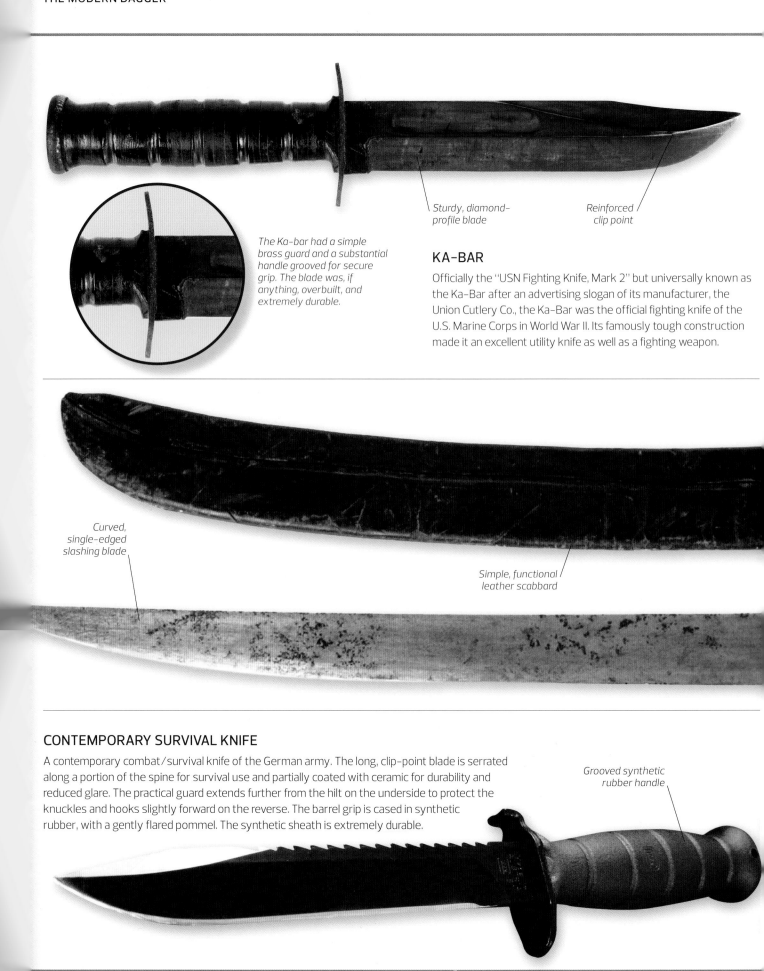

The Ka-bar had a simple brass guard and a substantial handle grooved for secure grip. The blade was, if anything, overbuilt, and extremely durable.

Sturdy, diamond-profile blade

Reinforced clip point

KA-BAR

Officially the "USN Fighting Knife, Mark 2" but universally known as the Ka-Bar after an advertising slogan of its manufacturer, the Union Cutlery Co., the Ka-Bar was the official fighting knife of the U.S. Marine Corps in World War II. Its famously tough construction made it an excellent utility knife as well as a fighting weapon.

Curved, single-edged slashing blade

Simple, functional leather scabbard

CONTEMPORARY SURVIVAL KNIFE

A contemporary combat/survival knife of the German army. The long, clip-point blade is serrated along a portion of the spine for survival use and partially coated with ceramic for durability and reduced glare. The practical guard extends further from the hilt on the underside to protect the knuckles and hooks slightly forward on the reverse. The barrel grip is cased in synthetic rubber, with a gently flared pommel. The synthetic sheath is extremely durable.

Grooved synthetic rubber handle

Steel blade

Finely worked silver décor on sheath

GAUCHO KNIFE

This South American gaucho knife features the indigenous Quero Quero bird on both sides of the blade. It has a horse's head on the sheath along with a bull's head and a sheep's head, some cherries, and a jar with a spoon in it.

Gauchos are above all horsemen, so equestrian motifs often figure on their more elaborate blades and mountings. This silver horse's head is a prime example.

COLLINS MACHETE

US Marines and soldiers hacked their way through the dense jungles of the Pacific islands with the M1942 Collins machete. With an 18-inch blade, it replaced the 22-inch model previously issued to American forces in tropical areas.

HELL IN THE PACIFIC

In the Pacific Theatre of World War II, the US Marines had to face not only a determined enemy but also climates and terrain that were themselves formidable challenges. Utility knives and machetes were indispensable assets for negotiating the jungles and rough, steep declivities of Pacific islands.

The sturdy, riveted hilt construction was typical of the Collins Company, which was renowned for the quality of its machetes.

World War II Presentation Daggers

As many historians have noted, the appeal of fascism between the two world wars was partly aesthetic; both Italian and German fascists invoked aesthetically charged rituals and older traditions of martial discipline. The resulting political and military cultures featured considerable regalia, including presentation daggers. None were more striking and symbolically charged than those of the Nazi regime, which both mythologized itself and sought to inspire a sense of privilege and elitism in its military ranks. These knives remain highly sought after by collectors.

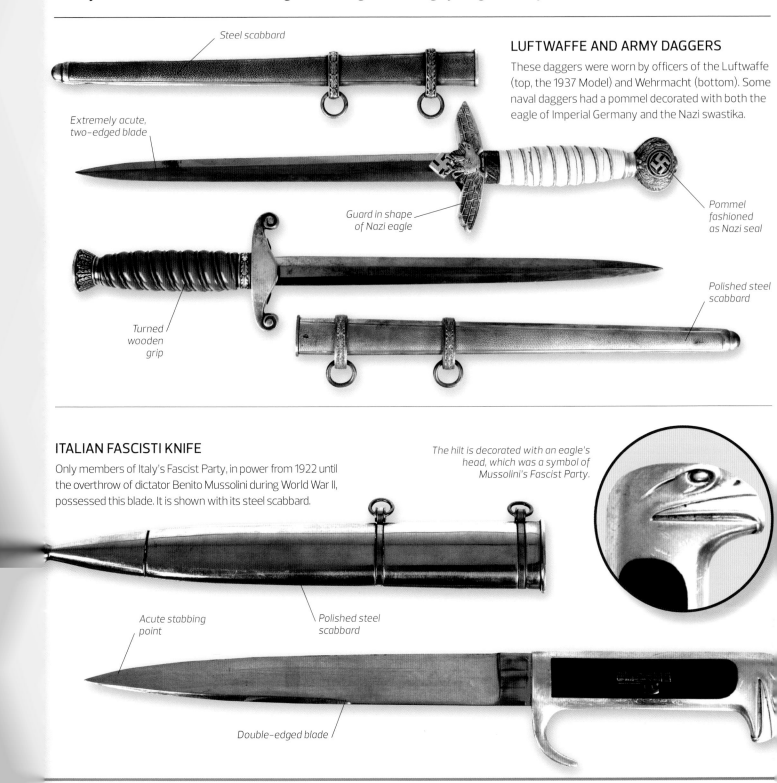

Steel scabbard

LUFTWAFFE AND ARMY DAGGERS

These daggers were worn by officers of the Luftwaffe (top, the 1937 Model) and Wehrmacht (bottom). Some naval daggers had a pommel decorated with both the eagle of Imperial Germany and the Nazi swastika.

Extremely acute, two-edged blade

Guard in shape of Nazi eagle

Pommel fashioned as Nazi seal

Turned wooden grip

Polished steel scabbard

ITALIAN FASCISTI KNIFE

Only members of Italy's Fascist Party, in power from 1922 until the overthrow of dictator Benito Mussolini during World War II, possessed this blade. It is shown with its steel scabbard.

The hilt is decorated with an eagle's head, which was a symbol of Mussolini's Fascist Party.

Acute stabbing point

Polished steel scabbard

Double-edged blade

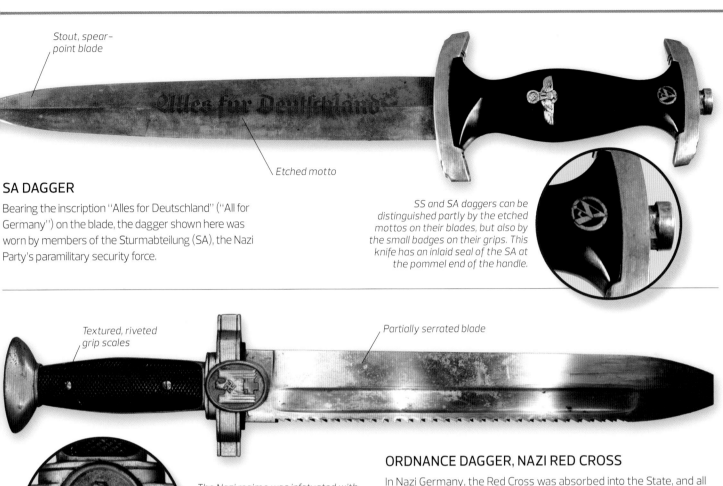

Stout, spear-point blade

Etched motto

SA DAGGER

Bearing the inscription "Alles for Deutschland" ("All for Germany") on the blade, the dagger shown here was worn by members of the Sturmabteilung (SA), the Nazi Party's paramilitary security force.

SS and SA daggers can be distinguished partly by the etched mottos on their blades, but also by the small badges on their grips. This knife has an inlaid seal of the SA at the pommel end of the handle.

Textured, riveted grip scales

Partially serrated blade

The Nazi regime was infatuated with ceremony, regalia, and heraldic devices. Even the Red Cross, an ostensibly apolitical organization, was co-opted into the Nazi hierarchy—a move signified by the subordination of the Red Cross symbol to the eagle and swastika on this seal.

ORDNANCE DAGGER, NAZI RED CROSS

In Nazi Germany, the Red Cross was absorbed into the State, and all the accoutrements that went into equipping this volunteer organization were blazoned with the Nazi eagle and swastika. This knife, symbolically shorn of its acute tip, is designed for the primary purpose of Red Cross work: assisting in civilian disaster relief. The two-edged blade is serrated on one side, and the guard and pommel are of the streamlined, pointedly modern and industrial look that was part of the Nazi aesthetic.

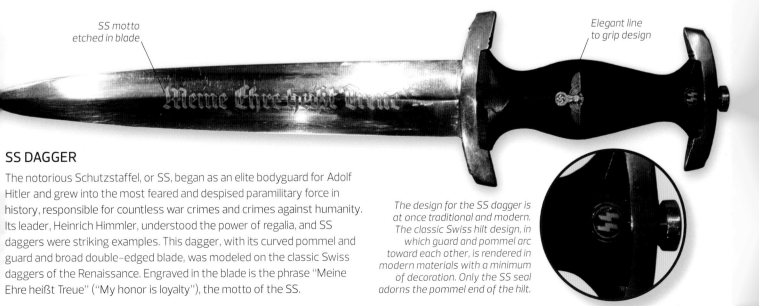

SS motto etched in blade

Elegant line to grip design

SS DAGGER

The notorious Schutzstaffel, or SS, began as an elite bodyguard for Adolf Hitler and grew into the most feared and despised paramilitary force in history, responsible for countless war crimes and crimes against humanity. Its leader, Heinrich Himmler, understood the power of regalia, and SS daggers were striking examples. This dagger, with its curved pommel and guard and broad double-edged blade, was modeled on the classic Swiss daggers of the Renaissance. Engraved in the blade is the phrase "Meine Ehre heißt Treue" ("My honor is loyalty"), the motto of the SS.

The design for the SS dagger is at once traditional and modern. The classic Swiss hilt design, in which guard and pommel arc toward each other, is rendered in modern materials with a minimum of decoration. Only the SS seal adorns the pommel end of the hilt.

Unusual Hand Weapons of the 20th Century

The exigencies of modern warfare and espionage, especially during the decades of the Cold War between the Soviet Union and the United States, gave rise to a bevy of unusual and highly purpose-specific blades. In addition, knives and the skills related to them took on a nostalgic cast, and knifemaking has become an artisanal activity, often devoted to producing either expensive collectors' items or highly technical tools and combat weapons, including throwing knives. This selection of interesting and unusual knives represents only some of the great variety of blades produced over the past few decades.

Hollow, nail-like point

Simple round end for grip

OSS COFFIN-NAIL DAGGERS

This hollow steel blade was designed to fit into tiny spaces, such as pens, pencils, or the seams of clothes. It was used by OSS employees during World War II.

Fake pen housing with pocket clip

Swivel mounting like that of a butterfly knife

SILVER PEN DAGGER

Writing implements, such as this American silver-cased pen, were used in espionage during the World War II and Cold War eras for hiding weapons.

Tough, riveted leather sheath

The serrated, concave portion of the knife's blade ensured a natural, effective slicing motion for cutting parachute cords and other materials. It could be used easily by feel as well as sight.

Concave utility blade

SOVIET PARATROOPER KNIFE

This unusual knife was invaluable to Soviet paratroopers. Its spoon-shaped, serrated, double-edged blade was primarily intended for quick and effective cutting of parachute shroud lines in the event of emergency, such as being tangled or hung in a tree after landing. The hilt is simple, with a pair of hardwood scales riveted to the tang. Though its rounded point is unsuitable for stabbing, in a desperate situation this blade could be used for combat.

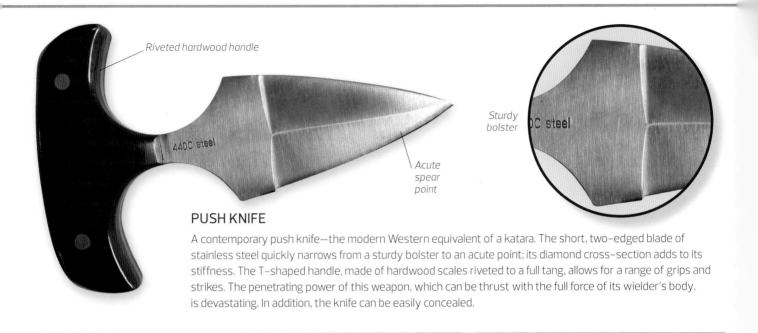

Riveted hardwood handle

Sturdy bolster

440C steel

OC steel

Acute spear point

PUSH KNIFE

A contemporary push knife—the modern Western equivalent of a katara. The short, two-edged blade of stainless steel quickly narrows from a sturdy bolster to an acute point; its diamond cross-section adds to its stiffness. The T-shaped handle, made of hardwood scales riveted to a full tang, allows for a range of grips and strikes. The penetrating power of this weapon, which can be thrust with the full force of its wielder's body, is devastating. In addition, the knife can be easily concealed.

Dramatically curved lines on handle and blade

Throwing knife with clip-point blade

Minimalist spear-point design

COLLECTION OF CONTEMPORARY THROWING KNIVES

Knife throwing has been practiced for centuries as a combat skill, art, and spectacle. These purpose-specific blades are designed to fly reliably using a range of different throwing grips. Their blades come in a variety of profiles, including clip points and drop points as well as spear points and spikes. As throwing weapons, they are designed strictly for balance in flight, and therefore have minimal, if any, mountings.

The manufacturer's mark on this throwing knife identifies it as the Ziel (German for "target") sport throwing knife, designed by John Bailey and manufactured by the German firm Boker. Bailey's signature is etched in the blade.

About the Berman Museum

Since the Berman Museum of World History opened its doors to the public in April of 1996, thousands of visitors have enjoyed its unique and varied collection of art, historical objects, and weapons. Located in the Appalachian foothills in Anniston, Alabama, and next door to the 75-year-old Anniston Museum of Natural History, which is affiliated with the Smithsonian, the Berman Museum's reputation and collection have grown exponentially since its inception. The Berman Museum's holdings number 8,500 objects and it has 3,000 items related to world history exhibited in its galleries. Among the many rare and fascinating objects from around the world, there are items such as an air rifle from Austria, military insignia from German and Italy, a scimitar from the Middle East, and graphically carved kris holders from Indonesia. The Museum attracts both a global and regional audience. All who visit can appreciate the historic significance of the collection and gain greater awareness and respect of other cultures.

Its five galleries—Deadly Beauty, American West, World War I, World War II, and Arts of Asia—exhibit items spanning a period of 3,500 years. A focal point of the Deadly Beauty gallery is the elaborate Royal Persian Scimitar, circa 1550, created for Abbas the Great, King of Persia. The American West gallery covers approximately 200 years (c. 1700–1900), emphasizing the United State's political, economic, social, and cultural structures, and their influences on settling the West.

The World War galleries use objects from the Museum collection to explore the causes and conditions of both wars, the historical significance of the countries involved, and the resulting political, economic, cultural, and social changes brought about by each war.

A rare piece of equipment in the World War I gallery is the Tanker's Splinter Goggles, used by tank personnel to protect their eyes and faces from metal splinters from machine-gun fire. Exhibited in the World War II gallery is the M1942 "Liberator" Pistol, as well as a large collection of Adolf Hitler's tea and coffee service, purported to have come from the last bunker that the Führer occupied. The Arts of Asia exhibit features an extensive and ever-growing collection of Asian textiles, ceramics, sculpture, jade, and metal.

The Berman Museum of World History is home to the vast and eclectic collection of Colonel Farley L. Berman and his wife, Germaine. Farley Berman, a lifelong resident of Anniston, Alabama, served in the European theater during World War II, and in the occupation force afterward. There he met Germaine, a French national. They were married and spent the next 50 years traveling the world acquiring historic weapons and artifacts, paintings, bronzes, and other works of art. Berman's self-trained collector's eye recognized the importance of items that were perhaps seen as ordinary, and he made it his mission to preserve a few. The Bermans established contacts—and a reputation—in numerous auction houses and among antique dealers in Europe and America.

The Bermans freely shared their collection with the public long before the City of Anniston constructed the Museum facility. Hundreds of military dignitaries and others were invited to their home for personal tours of their collection. Colonel Berman could best be described as a colorful storyteller and was notorious for firing blank rounds from his collection of spy weapons when guests least expected. He advised aspiring collectors to purchase good reference books, spend some years reading, and visit a range of museums before acquiring.

During the early 1990s, several large museums expressed interest in receiving the Bermans' collection. They were disappointed when Germaine proposed that the collection remain in Anniston. Colonel and Mrs. Berman's collection stands as the core of Berman Museum. Since the Museum's opening, many have recognized its importance and have contributed their own personal treasures to this impressive collection.

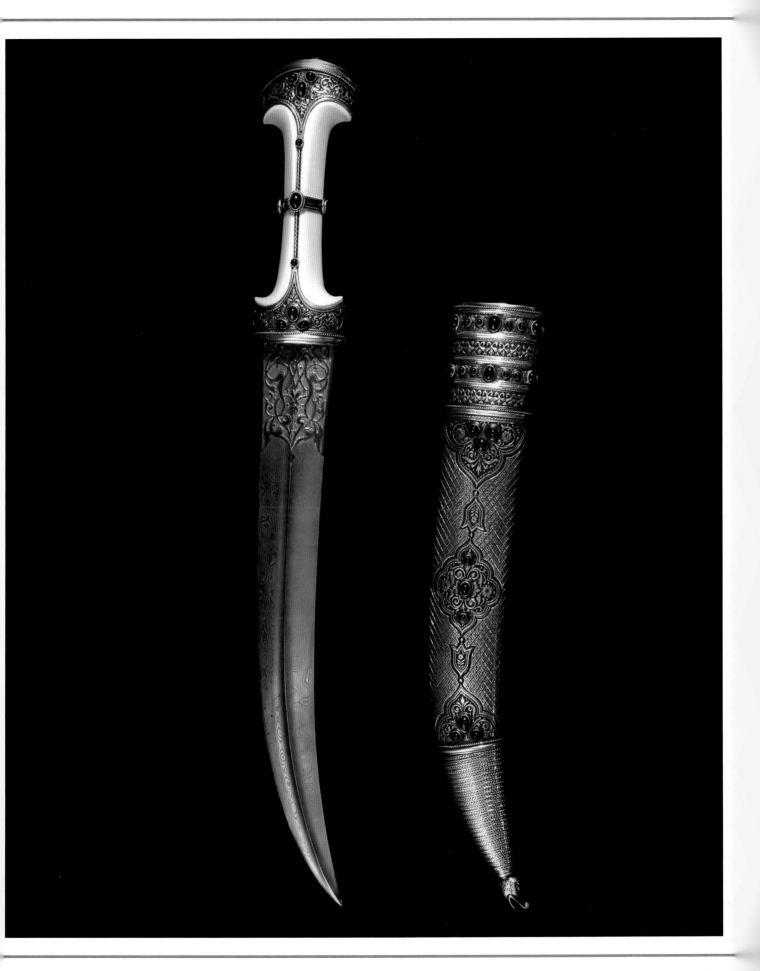

IVORY PHURBA

Page 105

CHINESE IMPERIAL
DAGGER

Page 97

Glossary of Knife Terms

A

adze A heavy cutting tool with an axe–like blade attached at right angles to a wooden handle

anodization An electrochemical process which adds color to titanium, which is especially conducive to this coloring process. Depending on the voltage used, colors can vary (high voltage = dark color, low voltage = light color)

B

belly The curved arc of the main blade. Especially useful for skinning knives as a large belly helps separate the skin and fat from internal organs without puncturing them with the point

bolster The portion of the handle that surrounds and strengthens the pivot. Traditionally, bolsters were metal but now they are often made of many other materials. On larger knives the bolster serves to balance the knives as well

Bowie knife A blade with an upswept, curving tip that is double-edged near the point. It is named for Colonel James Bowie who made this shape famous in the 19th century American west

butt The rear area of a knife. It might have a bolster, or a pommel, or an exposed tang, regardless the back end of the knife is the butt

C

chain mail Personal armor made of many links of iron or steel riveted together

choil The unsharpened section of a blade and the tang, typically located in front of the guard on the blade

clip point A common knife-blade shape with the appearance of having the forward third of the blade "clipped" off. The clip itself can be straight or concave

cutting edge (edge face) The sharpened, working section of a knife blade

D

dagger Short knife used for stabbing

Damascus steel Hot forged layers of soft and hard steel welded together with a visible grain or texture, which creates a swirled appearance

drop forged A process used in knife-making where hot metal is shaped within the walls of two dies

drop point A knife-blade shape where the spine slopes from the handle to the tip to increase the strength of the blade

double flat-ground A blade that is ground flat on both sides of the blade, tapering to an edge with no radius

F

ferrule A metal ring or cap placed over the end of a knife grip for added strength or stability

fighting knife, or combat knife Edged weapon intended for use in hand-to-hand combat rather than as a tool

finger groove Channels on the knife handle to accommodate fingers

flat ground A knife edge tapering from the cutting edge all the way to the blade's spine which is ground totally flat without a radius

forte The lower third of a blade, nearest the hilt, which is the strongest section of a blade

fuller (blood-groove) A channel or groove running down the middle of a blade. It is not designed as a blood channel or as a means to decrease suction when drawing a blade from a wound, as is often claimed. The fuller is actually an ingenious way of reducing the weight of the blade while not sacrificing strength

G

guard Vertical projections on a sword or knife, separating the hilt from the blade. Also known as crossguard

grabendoch German term for "trench dagger"

grip General term for the handle of a sword or knife. Typically made of a material that will both secure the hold and add a degree of cushioning for comfort

H

hammer forged The use of a hammer to shape a knife during the forging process

handguard A protrusion on a knife's handle, near the blade designed to protect a wielder's hand while parrying an opponent's blow. It ensures that the opponents blade doesn't slide down and injure the wielder's hand. Alternatively, it also protects a user by ensuring that their hand does not slide up onto the blade

handle The area where the knife is gripped

hilt The whole of the handle of a bladed weapon, usually consisting of the pommel, grip, and guard

hollow ground A concave, beveled edge that is generally sharper than a flat-ground blade but lighter and less durable

J

jambiya An Arabian curved dagger that was mostly decorative, but it was also an effective fighting knife

K

kindjal A curved double-edged fighting knife of the Cossacks

knap To break or chip (stone) with sharp blows, as in shaping flint or obsidian into tools

kriss, kris, or keris A traditional knife of Malaysia and Indonesia

kukri, or khukuri A Nepalese fighting knife

L,M,N

lanyard hole (thong hole) A hole placed in the end of a knife handle. Originally used by sailors who would place a cord through such a hole to keep from losing their knife overboard

luk Bend in a kris

main-gauche A dagger held in the left hand, used in conjunction with a sword in European sword fighting during the Renaissance

P,Q

partisan A type of pole arm with axe–heads below the blade that was used in Europe during the Middle Ages

patu A short-handled war club that was the principal weapon of the Maori people of New Zealand

pesh kabz A curved Persian knife used to penetrate chain-mail armor

plate armor Personal armor made of overlapping plates of iron or steel

point (tip) The distal front end of the blade, which determines the look and use of the knife

pommel The often knob-like projection atop a sword or knife. Although the pommel may be a highly decorative feature, it can also be crucial to a weapon's balance

quillon An "arm" on the handguard of sword, knife, or bayonet. It may be either straight or curved. A typical handguard comprises a pair of quillons of equal length, but some are more elaborate and asymmetrical. Some weapons (notably certain types of bayonet) may have a guard with a single quillon

R

ricasso The thick, non-ground part of the knife blade between the grinds and the bolsters.

rivets Pieces of metal or other material that secure the handle or bolsters to the tang

S

sabre, or saber Curved sword typically used by cavalry

scale A knife handle made of scales or slabs of material that are riveted, screwed, or bonded together.

scimitar Catch-all term for curved-bladed weapons of Middle Eastern origin

sheath Receptacle for carrying a knife

spine (back) Unsharpened side of the blade opposite of the cutting edge

swedge (false edge) An unsharpened bevel on the spine or back of the blade usually toward the tip. The swedge can be sharpened to create a double edge.

T,U

tanto A Japanese dagger used by the samurai

tang An extension of the blade to which the hilt is attached. The tang usually narrows dramatically in relation to the blade itself to accommodate the grip, and it often includes holes so that the grip can be secured using rivets

thumb ramp (thumb rest, thumb rise) The extended profile portion of the knife that accommodates the thumb. The thumb ramp helps the thumb apply pressure, guiding the knife in the cut

Y

yataghan A major blade weapon of the Ottoman Empire from the 15th through the 19th centuries

Index

Acknowledgments

Moseley Road Inc would like to thank the following people for their assistance and patience in the making of this book: **The Berman Museum of World History**: Adam Cleveland, David Ford, Susan Doss, Evan Prescott, Sara Prescott, Quinton Turner and Kira Tidmore

Picture Credits

Unless otherwise noted, all silhouetted weaponry images are from the Berman Museum of World History, Anniston, Alabama, and photographed by *f*-stop fitzgerald and Jonathan Conklin Photography, Inc., with the exception of the following:

KEY : a above, b below, l left, r right, c center, t top

coverl and coverc www.myarmoury.com coverr © shutterstock.com/Micha Klootwijk; 6r Opodeldok 7tc Wolfgang Sauber 7r Daderot 8r Binh Giang 9t Luis García 9b Skoklosters slott 10 Anagoria 12–13, 14l Didier Descouens 15t Opodeldok 15c Kim Bach/ Achird 15br Roland zh 15bl Wolfgang Sauber 16–17 Los Angeles County Museum of Art 18t Pasicles 18c E Petersen/ Shutterstock 18b BabelStone 20–21,22l Rémih 23t Claire H. 23br Los Angeles County Museum of Art 24t Los Angeles County Museum of Art 24b Daderot 25l, r Los Angeles County Museum of Art 26l, r, 27 Binh Giang 28 Noumenon 29 Los Angeles County Museum of Art 30–31 Los Angeles County Museum of Art 32–33 Los Angeles County Museum of Art 34–35 Los Angeles County Museum of Art 36–37 Los Angeles County Museum of Art 38t Phso2 38b παρακάτω 38r Norbert Nagel 39ca Wolfgang Sauber 39t Bernard Gagnon 39b MatthiasKabel 40t Luis García 40c Rama 41t Johnbod 41ca Rosemania 41br Wolfgang Sauber 43b Portable Antiquities Scheme 43c Binh Giang 43tl Nastya Pirieva 43tr foolonthehill/istockphoto 42b© BrokenSphere/Wikimedia Commons 44–45, 46l National Gallery, London 47b Günter Seggebäing 48t Lokilech 48c Hmaag 48b Sandstein 49t McLeod 49b Dbachmann 50 Livrustkammaren 51 the Mary Rose Trust 52 Walker Art Gallery 53b Shakko 53t Rama 56–57 Livrustkammaren 58t Walters Art Museum 58b Anagoria 59t Skoklosters slott 59c, b Livrustkammaren 60 Livrustkammaren 61 McLeod 64t Лапоть 65t Tim Avatar Bartel 65ca Лапоть 66–67, 68l Richard Bartz 69cb Macukali 69b Livrustkammaren 70t Daderot 70c, b J. Patrick Fischer 71t Walters Art Museum 71br J. Patrick Fischer 71bl Los Angeles County Museum of Art 74br Livrustkammaren 75cr Bernard Gagnon76, 77t J. Patrick Fischer 77b Hákon jarl 78b, 79c Jastrow 80, 81t Los Angeles County Museum of Art 81b Daderot 83t Los Angeles County Museum of Art 84t Jastrow 84b Los Angeles County Museum of Art 85t Jastrow 85b Livrustkammaren 90t Jastrow 102 Walters Art Museum 103 Daderot 104t Walters Art Museum 104b, 105 Los Angeles County Museum of Art 106–107 Los Angeles County Museum of Art 110t Los Angeles County Museum of Art 110cb, b Samuraiantiqueworld 111t PHGCOM 111b Samuraiantiqueworld 112–113, 114l Rept0n1x 115b Daderot 116–117 Brooklyn Museum 118 Vassil 119 Livrustkammaren 121t J. Patrick Fischer 121b Naval History & Heritage Command 124l Daderot 124r Shonagon 125t Los Angeles County Museum of Art 125c Simon Burchell 125b Hiart 127t Herwig Simons 127b New Guinea Tribal Art 133t Shakko 135r Livrustkammaren 137t George Shuklin 137b Olemac/ Shutterstock 138t Olemac/Shutterstock 138b Los Angeles County Museum of Art 142bl Claire H. 145t Carter Cutlery 147br Imperial War Museum 148b Wolfdale45 149b USMC 151b, c Rama 152b, 153t George Chernilevsky 153tl National Archives 153b www.knifethrowing.info 155 Sibrikov Valery/Shutterstock